Extraordinary Jesus

Ignite Your Season of Miracles

A 40-Day Devotional Bible Study in the Gospel of Luke

Dave Holland

Copyright Information

ISBN: 978-0-578-80001-1

Extraordinary Jesus

DEDICATION

To Jonie–my love, my wife, my inspiration, my life-partner

SPECIAL THANKS

To Susan Neal and all the folks at Word Weavers who patiently helped me become a better writer. My editor and friend, Vincent F. A. Golphin, improved this work. His insights made this work clear and relevant.

IN MEMORIAM

In loving memory of Justin 'Sky' Womack and Sheldon Womack

Additional Resources by Dave Holland

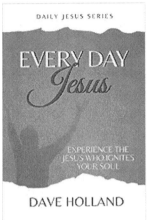

You can learn more about Dave and his books by going to Daveholland.org. Join his email list and you will receive a free gift along with access to his blog.

Contents

EXTRAORDINARY DAY 1

Extraordinary Adventure

He said to Simon, "Put out into deep water, and let down the nets for a catch." LUKE 5:4

They hunt, they conquer, and they eat like real men. Don't mess with Will, Oli, and Aiden when they are on a mission. Those 8- to 11-year-old boys patrol our neighborhood with the prowess of prehistoric hunters. Their thirst for adventure, especially in the murky woods at the end of our cul-de-sac, led them to a discovery.

The previous Friday night thieves vandalized Will and Oli's dad's truck. His backpack, containing critical medical equipment, and his cell phone was stolen. It was terrible. Their dad, an Air Force officer, and a Christian experienced several setbacks in his life. I saw him surrender his heavy heart to the Lord at the altar that Sunday.

On Monday, the boys were on the prowl in the woods searching for adventure and randomly discovered the stolen items. The conquering heroes not only found the backpack with all its contents, but they also recovered the cell phone. More importantly, that development lifted their dad's heart and encouraged his faith. The boys strutted around the neighborhood like peacocks for days until they moved on in their hunger for another escapade.

This same sense of hunger in the hunt is key to Christian living. Discovering the truth for your life feeds your soul in immense ways. When a believer searches for the truth they will find it and their confidence in their faith grows.

Hebrews 5:12-13 shows:

> *Though by this time you ought to be teachers, you need someone to teach you the elementary truths of God's word all over again. You need milk, not solid food! Anyone who lives on milk, being still an infant, is not acquainted with the teaching about righteousness. But solid food is for the mature, who by constant use have trained themselves to distinguish good from evil.*

Bodybuilder/actor Arnold Schwarzenegger echoed this scripture when he said, "Milk is for babies." Milk can nourish infants of mammals. Meat, on the other hand, must be hunted, gutted, butchered, and broiled. Meat feeds adults, people who want to grow strong.

Christians need spiritual protein to grow up and become everything God created them to be. They want to hunt for the meat of the Word of God, chew it, and digest it by thinking about the depths of God's Word rather than settling for milk.

Like Will, Oli, and Aiden believers must have the courage to venture forth despite a lack of knowledge. Christians have the mission to seek spiritual food.

Extraordinary Jesus is a guidebook for meat-hunters. Those who hunger to know Jesus every day need to track Christ's journeys, miracles, and teachings. They need to digest those truths to feed themselves and grow into mature believers.

The quest begins with reading the Gospel of Luke each day, paragraph by paragraph. Luke wrote the gospel for us who live under the influence of the Greco-Roman western world. Unique among Bible writers, Luke was a Gentile like us. Educated as a physician, but acting more like a historian, Luke researched every facet of Christ's life. He wrote for the benefit of his Gentile readers and his Greek mentor, Theophilus, whose name means lover of God.

This study focuses on Luke 5-9, which recounts the height of Christ's miracle-working period. Set in the region of Galilee, his popularity soars as he heals the sick, raises the dead, and delivers the oppressed. Those remarkable displays of God's presence among people stirred the heart of a nation and will stimulate yours.

Extraordinary Jesus adds some explanations and stories to help believers relate its ancient truths to our contemporary culture. Each chapter ends with a short prayer. The daily reflection requires less than fifteen minutes for the average reader.

Join Luke as he excavates truths that will set you free and unlocks principles that will transform you into a world-changer. Luke 5-9 begins with Jesus pushing Peter out into deeper water. There are miracles out there. Jesus urges Peter to fish where the big fish are abundant. I believe the Lord is calling us to impact the world in a big way through our lives and our witness.

I don't want to settle for little fish. And I sure don't want to live off milk. Join me on a hunting expedition for the Jesus that turned the world upside down. Capture the meat of God's Word by wrestling with it, doing what it says, and engaging the power of its message. Recapture your childhood sense of adventure like Will, Oli, and Aiden. You will discover truths that empower your life. Knowing Jesus is an adventure that you need to hunt down and grapple with until it becomes part of you.

Dear Lord, I have played it safe for far too long. Push me out into the deep, Lord, where the big fish are. It may be dangerous, but I want the thrill of seeing you do the impossible. Use this devotional to challenge me to chew the scriptures. I want to digest these truths for my life. Bless this meat I am about to partake. Help me explore the grounds of your grace, the vastness of your

Extraordinary Jesus

*love, and the potential of your power. In Christ's name,
I pray, amen.*

The Healing Touch

While Jesus was in one of the towns, a man came along who was covered with leprosy. When he saw Jesus, he fell with his face to the ground and begged him, "Lord, if you are willing, you can make me clean." Jesus reached out his hand and touched the man. "I am willing," he said. "Be clean!" And immediately the leprosy left him. Then Jesus ordered him, "Don't tell anyone, but go, show yourself to the priest and offer the sacrifices that Moses commanded for your cleansing, as a testimony to them." Yet the news about him spread all the more, so that crowds of people came to hear him and to be healed of their sicknesses. But Jesus often withdrew to lonely places and prayed. Luke 5:12–16

My wife of twenty-eight years walked out on me, our home, and our family sixteen years ago. I was devastated by my failure. An ugly divorce followed not long after. It was the darkest period of my life as loneliness, lust, and depression ravaged my soul. I felt like a dead man walking.

As I considered the prospect of growing old alone, the future looked like a hollow, dismal pit of despair. Out of my emotional emptiness, something within me cried out, Will I ever feel a loving touch again?

Look at your hands. Run your fingers over your palm, your skin, your fingertips. You have the power to heal or destroy. The choice is yours. You can touch and comfort hurting people, or you can withhold your embrace and condemn them to silent suffering.

Luke's passage above reveals in startling colors Christ's great compassion. Walk with Jesus along the dusty Galilean road as a man rotting with leprosy approaches and the human drama unfolds. The leper suffers from a wretched disease that slowly strangles his nervous system. Dying nerve endings choke off his sense of touch. His fingers and toes rot and fall off. The tip of his nose and his ears slowly decay and disfigure him. In those days, the law commanded that such a person quarantine from their community, home, and family. Condemned to die a hideous death in a leper colony, he would never feel human touch again.

Leprosy, in that ancient culture, bore moral and religious stigmas. The disease impacts a person at every level of their being—spirit, soul, and body. People with leprosy were considered contagious and cursed by God. Religion-imposed rules forbade the infected to enter their homes or touch their spouses and children. By law, if any person came near to a leper, the diseased person had to cry out, "Unclean, unclean!" Lepers could not even worship at synagogues. Most felt utterly lost, alienated from God.

In Luke's gospel, loneliness drapes the leper like a wet, stinking garment. Feeling angry at his circumstances and the heartbreaking loss of his future, he approaches Christ and begs for healing.

What did he have to lose? Life couldn't get any worse.

"If you are willing you can make me clean," he pleads.

Jesus then breaks the law--wrecks the rules--and embarrasses the religious scholars. He reaches out and touches the leper. Everyone gasps. He speaks the word of healing, and power flows. He didn't have to touch him. Christ could have healed him and moved on without touching the leper's stench and rottenness, but the Lord touches him to heal the depths of his soul.

You may not have the ability to cure leprosy, but by faith in Jesus Christ, you have the power to heal people's hearts with a loving touch. Many feel the leprosy of divorce, abuse, widowhood, or a host of other human afflictions. You have the power to reach out and touch someone in Christ's name.

Human touch is medicine for the heart. Its healing properties penetrate the exterior shell that hurt feelings and loneliness create. How many people walk through life with a familiar façade while inwardly crying out for someone to love them? Won't somebody touch my aching heart?

Father God, I need your touch upon my life. Life has left me battered and torn, but I turn to you, the source of my restoration. Yours is the touch that heals. Your name calms my fears and settles my emotions. People may hurt me, say rude things, or criticize, but I put my trust in your loving touch today. Give me the courage to speak your name to the hurting. Help me to reach out in faith to those who need your touch. Amen.

What Do You Do When You Get Busy?

But Jesus often withdrew to lonely places and prayed. Luke 5:16

The busier Jesus got, the more he prayed. Will you pull aside with Jesus to talk with God?

We tend to pray less when we're stressed, and the fire of our faith slowly grows cold. The result is a lukewarm faith that remembers how to act godly but inwardly stagnates.

As a pastor, I always found Sundays draining. Many people received ministry. Some needed special attention, and a host of people came from hurting places in their lives. Church often left me exhausted. One Sunday at about 2 p.m., I finally headed home from the church. I crashed for a brief rest and woke up at 5 p.m. to realize I missed a monthly responsibility to minister at a nursing home. Later, the activities director at the nursing home called and mentioned that the previous three ministers overlooked their service as well. Guilt clung to me like skunk spray.

I prayed that the Lord would forgive me, and of course, he did. I asked myself, Have I grown so complacent that I would miss an opportunity to minister to people who do not have the opportunity to go to church? Are believers today so caught up in church programs that they overlook those who are most vulnerable? Have we lost our zeal for the Lord?

We enjoy the good life here in America and are especially vulnerable to complacency. Jesus confronts us with a solemn judgment:

> *I know your works, that you are neither cold nor hot. I could wish you were cold or hot. So then, because you are lukewarm, and neither cold nor hot, I will vomit you out of My mouth. (Revelation 3:15-18, NKJV)*

Jesus shows us a better way. He withdraws to be alone when he is weary. No Facebook, no texts, no cell phones, no tweets, no LinkedIn or hooking up, simply alone with God.

Knowing how to be solitary is central to the art of living and loving. Healthy time alone with God helps us to dip into the well of God's great grace. We perceive God's love and acceptance, and it helps us then be accepting and loving toward others. Being present with God enables us to be fully present with others.

If you take the time to lower the external noise in your life, you will hear the whispers of God. Follow their lead and you will rock your world.

My dear friend, Pat, shared a dream with me. She walked through a beautiful green meadow crowned with a shimmering blue sky. The woman felt an intermittent balmy breeze as she drew near to a gently flowing river. As she did, she saw a distant shepherd approach from the other side.

As the distance narrowed between the two travelers, Pat saw the shepherd's lips move as if he were speaking but could not hear the sound. She called, "I can't hear you." The shepherd pointed down at the river. Pat drew near to the water. She faintly heard some of the sounds that he spoke but could not make out the words. Pat became desperate as she became aware that this Shepherd was Jesus.

"Lord, I still can't hear you," she cried. From the far side of the river, the Shepherd pointed down to the water again. He knelt by the shoreline, then called out to her.

Pat knelt with her ear next to the water, listened with all her might and said, "Lord, I want to hear Your voice."

Then, she heard the most beautiful sound. The Shepherd called her name. Pointing to the water again, he said, "This is how hard you have to listen to hear Me."

Dear friends, take the time to get down by the water alone with God. Listen quietly for His voice.

Extraordinary Jesus

He will give you peace and direct your life into healthy, prosperous pathways. Allow me to end with this challenge—set aside seven minutes a day to be quiet before God. Wherever you are, whatever you are doing, just stop. Take seven minutes of silence—don't talk, don't think, don't ask. Just be with Jesus. Those seven minutes will rock your world.

God save me from the curse of the lukewarm person. May you forgive me for my sin of busyness and lead me to the wilderness with you. Give me the discipline to stop and be with you. Help me to kneel close to the water. May I hear your voice, O Lord, and know real intimacy with You. Jesus, empower me to listen to your voice and learn your ways.

Extraordinary Faith

One day as he was teaching, Pharisees and teachers of the law, who had come from every village of Galilee and from Judea and Jerusalem, were sitting there. And the power of the Lord was present for him to heal the sick. Some men came carrying a paralytic on a mat and tried to take him into the house to lay him before Jesus. When they could not find a way to do this because of the crowd, they went up on the roof and lowered him on his mat through the tiles into the middle of the crowd, right in front of Jesus.

When Jesus saw their faith, he said, "Friend, your sins are forgiven."

The Pharisees and the teachers of the law began thinking to themselves, "Who is this fellow who speaks blasphemy? Who can forgive sins but God alone?"

Jesus knew what they were thinking and asked, "Why are you thinking these things in your hearts? Which is easier: to say, 'Your sins are forgiven,' or to say, 'Get up and walk'? But that you may know that the Son of Man has authority on earth to forgive sins. ..." He said to the paralyzed man, "I tell you, get up, take your mat and go home." Immediately he stood up in front of them, took what he had been lying on and went home praising God. Everyone was amazed and gave praise to God. They were filled with awe and said, "We have seen remarkable things today." Luke 5:17–26

Recently I visited a woman in the hospital who suffered unbearable pain. Cancer wreaked mayhem throughout her body. Buzzers were beeping and monitors flashing while she tossed and turned seeking a position that would alleviate her agony. Judging by the way she acted, her pain meds ebbed way too low.

In the chair next to her bed, sat her husband, immobilized, not knowing what to do about his wife's pain. "What are they doing for her?" I asked.

Staring blanking into the distance, he replied, "Nothing, absolutely nothing."

So, I threw a hissy fit at the nurse's station and got someone to address her situation. They called the doctor immediately and left a voicemail, small comfort to a person in agony. Finally, it occurred to me to anoint her with oil and pray in the name of the Lord. Jesus is our great physician with the power to bring comfort and healing.

Christ encountered a similar situation in Luke 5:17-26, but with much better results. His disciples and religious scholars surrounded him. Together with a doting crowd, they crammed into a small home. Four people with a friend in desperate pain were outside trying to get to Jesus, the healing rabbi. In their efforts to bring their friend to Jesus, they went up to the flat roof of that ancient Middle Eastern house. The friends began to hack through its thatched-mud roof. They dug through a covering two feet thick with muck, twigs, and rafters. It was no easy chore to lower a full-grown man on a stretcher into the midst of the crowd below. Nothing would deny them the presence of the Lord.

Christ not only healed the man, but he also forgave his sins.

Why was this man healed while others in Israel continued to suffer?

Indeed the compassion of Christ extends to all who are distressed. The difference was that man had friends who would overcome any obstacle to enter the presence of Jesus. Their faith compelled them to get him where the power of the Lord to heal was present. May God give us such persistent friends.

Loving ministry and spiritual break-through always have significant, seemingly impossible obstacles. For instance, Jesus taught us to go the extra mile in serving our oppressors, even to turn the other cheek when struck by an enemy. God seems to make His presence known in the extra mile rather than merely in the ordinary. Jesus would not deny the kind of faith that would lower a friend down through a roof into a room so that Christ would heal him.

Some barriers confront us every day, tests designed to strengthen our faith. It was difficult for these people to get their needy friend to Jesus. Still, they did the work necessary to overcome the obstacle.

This passage begs the question, "how many Christians today would overcome obstacles to bring a friend to Christ?" Lifeway Research recently conducted a survey showing that 78 percent of non-Christian people would listen if someone shared what they believed about Jesus.

How many Christians even ask God for healing? We have not because we ask not. Our faith wavers like the waves of the sea because we avoid difficult situations. May God give us what Charles Price called the Real Faith that hears God's whispers and obeys His promptings. Then we would see God's handiwork.

I went home after anointing my friend at the hospital with oil. Her husband said later that she began to get better from the moment I put that stuff (oil) on her head and prayed. Two days later, they moved her to a nursing home for physical therapy. She still has cancer to fight and to overcome the last enemy, death, but the Lord has surely carried her sorrow and pain away.

Heavenly Father, I ask you to strengthen me to act in faith like these men who dug through the roof for their friend. May you give me extraordinary faith, not only to believe for healing, but also for forgiveness for the sinners that I meet. I confess that you are both the great physician and the great forgiver. Amen.

Leaving Money on the Table

After this, Jesus went out and saw a tax collector by the name of Levi sitting at his tax booth. "Follow me," Jesus said to him, and Levi got up, left everything and followed him.

Then Levi held a great banquet for Jesus at his house, and a large crowd of tax collectors and others were eating with them. But the Pharisees and the teachers of the law who belonged to their sect complained to his disciples, "Why do you eat and drink with tax collectors and 'sinners'?"

Jesus answered them, "It is not the healthy who need a doctor, but the sick. I have not come to call the righteous, but sinners to repentance.
Luke 5:27–32

We hate paying taxes. Americans revolted against the British Empire and started a war because we felt the tariffs were unfair. In ancient Palestine, people despised Tax Collectors for their greed and because they added arbitrary expenses to a person's levy.

As slaves of the Roman Empire, they had no say or recourse in the amount they were taxed. Local tax collectors made themselves wealthy by charging exorbitant fees. They were hated for this practice and were classed together with robbers, thieves, and prostitutes.

Dr. Luke recounts the story of Christ passing by Levi, the tax collector, with the simple invitation, "Follow me." Overjoyed at the Master's attention, Levi leaves the tax money on the table and walks away from it.

Levi then throws a big party at his home, inviting all his friends. Luke uses the Greek word mega to describe the enormous celebration. Jesus eats, drinks, and talks with these disreputable people—at home with sinners as well as saints. Not far away, fully aghast with Christ's behavior, sit the austere Pharisees.

"Why do you eat with tax collectors and sinners?" They gasp with thinly veiled horror. They asked, "Why do you eat and drink with such scum?" (Luke 5:30, NLT.) Jesus saw something in Levi that the self-righteous Pharisees didn't.

There is no instance in Scripture where a religious traditionalist reacts with the enthusiasm that Levi does. Levi acts like a freshly forgiven believer who invites all his friends to meet Jesus. In contrast, the Pharisees gathered to criticize Christ. The difference was in their response to the Lord–Levi reacts with joy. At the same time, the religious people reek with the smell of suspicion.

Jesus concludes the passage in Luke 5:32, NLT, "I have come to call sinners to turn from their sins, not to spend my time with those who think they are already good enough." Jesus comes to lead a world estranged from God back to the Father. The sick need a physician, and he came to impart health and direction back to God. The tax collector listened and followed Christ, drawing in his wayward friends into his journey with the Lord, and he was happy.

Sinners benefit from the awareness of their distance from God, while religious people clothe their cold hearts with ritualistic behaviors. The telltale sign is their constant suspicion and criticism of others. We share this inherited blindness induced by sin's dense fog. Levi had the self-awareness to share the joy of his new-found freedom while the Pharisee remained trapped in the cell of his self-righteousness. He couldn't bring himself to be happy for a sinner finding forgiveness.

The Pharisee shows us that a critical spirit isolates us from the party. Judgmentalism condemns us to the smallness of our thinking. Christ is feasting and drinking the joy of a redeemed sinner while the religious man is sucking on the sour lemon of legalism. The Pharisee, stuck in his cold, religious routine, missed the visitation of God.

The transformation in Levi was so profound that Luke says, "he left everything and followed Him."

Picture this–Levi, the Tax Collector, operating his table in the town square, demanding taxes from everyone as Jesus approaches. Levi's record books and money are sitting on the table when Jesus calls to him, "Follow me." Levi gets up and walks away from the table. He leaves the records and the co-erced money behind. Levi became a faithful follower of Christ.

The Pharisee could not grasp such a profound change in a person. Levi's friends were amazed by it. Heaven dances for joy. How many Christians are willing to leave the money on the table? This message is sobering for those who have been Christians for many years. Have we become stiff and unyielding, or are we ready to enter the party?

Lord Jesus, hear my cry today. I don't want to grow old and stale–angry that you would bless people who are different from me. Bring me into the beautiful meadow of your graciousness, help me to breathe the air of your kindness and generosity. Grant me the ability to be happy, even when you move outside of the box of my understanding. You are Lord, and you are good to people–help me walk in Your steps and attitude.

Lord God, I ask you to free me from anything that hinders me from following you. I pray that money will never hold me back from celebrating what you have done in my life. May I look with your eyes upon those who need you and show them compassion. In your name, I pray. Amen.

Making All Things New

They said to him, "John's disciples often fast and pray, and so do the disciples of the Pharisees, but yours go on eating and drinking."

Jesus answered, "Can you make the guests of the bridegroom fast while he is with them? But the time will come when the bridegroom will be taken from them; in those days they will fast."

He told them this parable: "No one tears a patch from a new garment and sews it on an old one. If he does, he will have torn the new garment, and the patch from the new will not match the old. And no one pours new wine into old wineskins. If he does, the new wine will burst the skins, the wine will run out and the wineskins will be ruined. No, new wine must be poured into new wineskins. And no one after drinking old wine wants the new, for he says, 'The old is better.'" Luke 5:33–39

Woven into the fabric of our lives are twists and knots that feel terrible. Pulled in directions we do not expect, and we feel stressed. These loops produce a larger tapestry than we can imagine. As we walk through the complicated webs of our lives, we feel tangled. Mysteriously, the Weaver at the beam has a grand design in mind.

The rhyme and reason of life are often hiding while we flail about building our nests. Our lack of control unnerves us with the haunting realization that Someone else is at the helm. The mess and grime of life scream at us that evil abounds and is about to crucify us. Then we discover that was the plan all along. No dying, no resurrection. You do not qualify for new life until you surrender and allow God to direct your steps.

The parable above was intended by the Lord to bring us clarity. Essentially, Jesus says the same thing in three different ways. First, no one sews a new patch of cloth to an old garment. Jesus did not come to repair the old covenant of living by rules, but rather to institute a new covenant of grace received through faith in Him.

God provided a new garment, Christ's righteousness, to cover our sin. People try to patch together their own character by continually repairing an old, tattered godliness image built on good works. The problem is that it never works because our sin nature, our inclination to sin, runs through every cell in our bodies. Most people just give up and settle for the false notion, I hope I'm good enough to make it to heaven.

The second part of the parable reaches us at a deeper level. No one puts new wine in old wineskins. While the metaphor is obscure to us, it was clear to Christ's listeners. The ancients commonly skinned animals before butchering them. The common practice was to sew the skin closed, making it capable of containing liquid, specifically grape juice. The grape juice expanded and contracted with such chaotic fermentation that it stretched the limits of the wineskin.

Once aged, the juice could be drunk as a delightful wine. As people poured wine from the skin, they needed to refill it immediately, or it would dry out and become useless. Christ's point—don't render yourself unusable by allowing your heart to remain empty and dry. God wants to pour new life into your heart—his word combined with the transforming power of the Holy Spirit.

At the close of his parable of the wineskins, Jesus put it this way, "And no one after drinking old wine wants the new, for he says, 'The old is better'" (Luke 5:39). It is easier to fall back to what is familiar and comfortable and justify that rather than launch out into a life guided by the Spirit.

Author Lisa Bevere says, "When God begins to do a new thing in a new way the greatest opposition comes from the old thing with its old ways!" The human-made rules of religion must not hinder the Gospel of the Kingdom. The Spirit must be free to work unfettered. The New Wine may not be smooth to the tongue and finely aged like old wine. It may be a bit sharp and unrefined, but it is alive. You can't contain it in old structures. You must find new wineskins for it.

In my words, Jesus concludes the matter by saying, you've been drinking old wine. Why would you want to drink new wine?" Only one reason— you're thirsty for a new life.

The Old Covenant dynamic is exhausted. Christ came to establish the New Covenant—to pour new wine into the wineskins of our lives and to release a day of transformative growth in us. You must start the growth process over, led by the Holy Spirit, giving fresh insight, new inspiration, and creative challenges. New garment, new wine, new wineskin. Behold, He makes all things new.

Lord, fill us full again with your new wine. This time help us to contain it and grow with it, rather than lose it through our stubbornness and inflexibility. Help me, Lord, to recognize the powerful new ways you want to work in my life. In Jesus' name, I pray. Amen.

Lord of Your Sunday

One Sabbath Jesus was going through the grainfields, and his disciples began to pick some heads of grain, rub them in their hands and eat the kernels. Some of the Pharisees asked, "Why are you doing what is unlawful on the Sabbath?"

Jesus answered them, "Have you never read what David did when he and his companions were hungry? He entered the house of God, and taking the consecrated bread, he ate what is lawful only for priests to eat. And he also gave some to his companions." Then Jesus said to them, "The Son of Man is Lord of the Sabbath."

On another Sabbath he went into the synagogue and was teaching, and a man was there whose right hand was shriveled. The Pharisees and the teachers of the law were looking for a reason to accuse Jesus, so they watched him closely to see if he would heal on the Sabbath. But Jesus knew what they were thinking and said to the man with the shriveled hand, "Get up and stand in front of everyone." So he got up and stood there.

Then Jesus said to them, "I ask you, which is lawful on the Sabbath: to do good or to do evil, to save life or to destroy it?"

He looked around at them all, and then said to the man, "Stretch out your hand." He did so, and his hand was completely restored. But they were furious and began to discuss with one another what they might do to Jesus.

Luke 6:1–11

The poison that killed Christ oozed from an ugly boil of self-righteous religion. The Pharisees hated Jesus because He challenged their traditions and exposed the pride enshrined in their creed. Their religion was the voice in their head whispering, *we're better than you because we're more religious.* God hates such pride.

Religious systems are constructed to shield us from dangerous doctrines and prevent our fallible flesh from stumbling. Yet, ritualized rules alienate us from God because we inevitably fail. Our guilt causes us to hide in shame. The Pharisees tightened the noose of legalism around the people's necks while Jesus showed them mercy.

Luke recounted when Christ and His disciples walked to the synagogue on the Sabbath. They were hungry, so the group ate kernels of wheat gleaned along the way. In their culture, this was normal. Deuteronomy 23:25 states, "If you enter your neighbor's grainfield, you may pick kernels with your hands." But this activity was forbidden by the Pharisees as a kind of harvesting work. They confronted Jesus on the violation of their rules.

Jesus responds with a curveball. He describes King David and his men going to the Tabernacle of God, who eat the showbread reserved for the priests. That was a violation of the Scriptures (I Samuel 21:6). Yet, David demonstrated that it is allowable to show mercy in the spirit of the Word. Further, Jesus revealed that He is Lord of the Sabbath, who chose compassion over the Law. Christ obliterated a pillar of their religion and replaced it with grace.

Jesus confirms the proclamation of His Lordship over the Sabbath by a mighty display of his mercy and power. Christ arrives at the synagogue where He faces angry Pharisees and strangely calls out a man in the crowd with a crippled hand telling him to "stand in front of everyone." Jesus then poses the question, "Is it lawful on the Sabbath to do good or to do evil, to save life or to destroy?" (Luke 6:9, NKJV). In the face of their haughty silence, Christ heals the man to confirm that the Sabbath is designed for good. The battle lines are drawn as the Pharisees walk away, "filled with rage."

God established the Sabbath day of rest for the restoration of our minds and bodies. After a hard week of labor, worship renews us and draws us to God. While enforcing their religion, the Pharisees lost sight of God's purpose for the Sabbath. The Sabbath blessing had become entrenched in rules so burdensome people forgot who God is—the source of life, truth, and mercy.

What about the man with the withered hand?

Angry with the legalist's awkward and powerless silence, Jesus instantly heals the shriveled hand. Uninhibited, undignified, irreligious joy erupted in the heart of that man. That is God's desire for us.

This passage begs the question--who is the Lord of our Sunday?

According to the National Football League, football is watched by more people on a typical Sunday than those who go to worship. Alcoholics Anonymous (AA) could say that more people turn to AA for help than those who attend church. I wonder if it is a fear of judgment that keeps people home. A living love for the Lord longs for worship and acts of mercy toward others.

Who is Lord of your Sunday?

Lord God, I want to follow Christ without the cancer of legalism. I long for the healing of others through your mercy. Forgive me when I judge others as if they earned their sad plight. When I make you, Lord of my Sabbath, worship restores my soul. In your name, I pray. Amen.

Chosen by God,
Excluded by People

Now it came to pass in those days that He went out to the mountain to pray, and continued all night in prayer to God. And when it was day, He called His disciples to Himself; and from them He chose twelve..." Luke 6:12–13, NKJV

The color and majesty of the Sistine Chapel rocked me. The beauty, pageantry, and sense of history in Rome ooze from every nook and cranny. The paintings and sculptures rival the greatest museums in the world. The sheer scope of Saint Peter's Basilica rising to a height of 448 feet, almost the size of the Washington Monument, and covering over 50,000 square feet made me feel small.

The gospel stories portrayed in the frescoes, on the other hand, drew me into the Biblical narratives like a bee drawn into a flower.

My wife and I scampered throughout the city, taking in the history and the sights. We toured many churches basking in the art of Raphael and Michelangelo. In one church, we happened upon a celebration of the Mass. We sat and enjoyed the worship as the ceremony unfolded. The priest asked for people to come forward to receive the Eucharist. My wife, Jonie, raised as a Catholic, suggested, "Let's go forward."

I was hesitant but agreed. I waited in line with hundreds of people and reminded myself that I wasn't Catholic. I believed differently than the other participants, yet my heart longed for more of Jesus. Inwardly I cried out, I want more of Jesus, and if I draw close to Him, He will draw near to me.

As I approached the altar, the priest saw my awkwardness. He asked in halting English, "Are you Catholic?"

I answered, "No."

He refused to offer me communion.

I understand why the priest denied me. Catholic rules only allow baptized Catholics to receive communion. Many Protestants would be aghast that I attempted to receive communion in a Catholic Church. The Scriptures guide my faith in the Lord. All who believe in the death, burial, and resurrection of Christ are Christians destined for heaven, 1 Corinthians 15:2-4:

> *By this gospel you are saved, if you hold firmly to the word I preached to you. Otherwise, you have believed in vain. For what I received I passed on to you as of first importance: that Christ died for our sins according to the Scriptures, that he was buried, that he was raised on the third day according to the Scriptures.*

Since Catholics also believe this, I consider them my brothers and sisters in the family of God. I long for the day when we can all gather at the Marriage Supper of the Lamb to celebrate the victory Jesus won for us.

All believers in Christ are chosen by God for salvation through "sanctification by the Spirit and belief in the truth" (2 Thessalonians 2:13). I am secure in who I am in God—a disciple of Christ, whom He has chosen (Ephesians 1:4). Though a priest or minister might exclude me from communion, the Lord never will. Jesus receives me, as the late gospel singer Mahalia Jackson sang, "just as I am without one plea, but that His blood was shed for me."

The sad fact remains that Christendom is divided. I still love, respect, and admire my Catholic brothers and sisters while I treasure my Protestant heritage and theology. But what will it take to bring us together? Will some tragedy or great persecution need to occur before we realize we have a common Lord? Is that what it will take before we come together in Christian fellowship? I hope not, but we have a long way to go.

Jesus gives us hope. He prayed all night in John 17:11 before the choice of his disciples. Also, Christ prayed all night before he left the disciples:

> *I will remain in the world no longer, but they are still in the world, and I am coming to you. Holy Father protect them by the power of your name— the name you gave me — so that they may be one as we are one, (John 17:11).*

This prayer of Christ is powerful and eternal. The Holy Spirit is still working to fulfill that prayer. A few years ago, during the Easter season, I felt led to walk each street in my town, praying for every home, family, and church. At each worship site, I would lay hands on the building, interceding for spiritual breakthrough. On some occasions, I got to pray for the pastors. But only one minister, Father Jim Golka from Saint Patrick's Catholic Church in North Platte, Nebraska, reciprocated by praying for me. Christ's prayer works one person at a time.

> *Bind us together, Lord, with chords that cannot be broken. Heal your wounded people and bring us together as one. We fight among ourselves, protecting our turf, and we gain nothing but strife and division. Forgive us for our history of conflict and bring us together for your glory, O God. Amen.*

Where the Ordinary Become Extraordinary

When morning came, he called his disciples to him and chose twelve of them, whom he also designated apostles: Simon (whom he named Peter), his brother Andrew, James, John, Philip, Bartholomew, Matthew, Thomas, James son of Alphaeus, Simon who was called the Zealot, Judas son of James, and Judas Iscariot, who became a traitor.

He went down with them and stood on a level place. A large crowd of his disciples was there and a great number of people from all over Judea, from Jerusalem, and from the coast of Tyre and Sidon, who had come to hear him and to be healed of their diseases. Those troubled by evil spirits were cured, and the people all tried to touch him, because power was coming from him and healing them all. Luke 6: 13–19

Jesus gathered 12 Disciples to walk with Him for three years. Christianity is now growing exponentially with numbers in the billions. How many actually walk with him?

Christ emerged from prayer on a mission to change the world. The first thing He did was appoint to apostles, literally "sent ones." The list of apostles started with Peter and ended with Judas the Betrayer. All were Galileans except Judas. They were country boys. Four fished for a living, one collected taxes, none were rich, famous, educated, well-connected, or notable. Not one was a scribe, scholar, priest, elder, or ruler. They were ordinary people.

One of the great glories of God's call is that our weakness becomes an opportunity for His power. Our ordinariness makes room for His extra-ordinariness. As Abraham Lincoln once drawled, "God must have liked ordinary people because He made so many of them."

Paul, the "Apostle come lately," did not fit the profile of the others. His family was wealthy. He was a Pharisee but renounced that status when God called him to follow. He, who was originally named Saul, after the proud Old Testament King, became

Paul, which in Latin, means "small" or "humble." Big Saul chose to become Small Paul!

The pivotal point in Luke 6 occurred when Jesus turned from calling His disciples to demonstrating the power of the Kingdom of God. Luke notes, "He went down with them and stood on a level place," to show that Jesus was a man of the people. The Lord walked among them, not above them. He saw them, felt them, touched them, and healed them.

The people came to hear Jesus, and healing was the by-product. Faith is born where the Word of God is shared. Jesus was present to heal all their diseases and to bear their sickness away. He knew their maladies would be beaten upon His back by the Romans. He would carry them into the throne room of His Father. Jesus took our weakness and carried our troubles away.

In the above passage, we see the people reach out to touch Christ. Luke uses the Greek word haptomai, meaning "to touch, attach oneself, or fasten." It is used in ancient literature to describe touching fire to kindling wood to start a hearth fire. We need to touch Jesus so we can catch fire with faith!

In this instance, Doctor Luke also employs the Greek word iaomai, a strong verb, to describe the "healing" power flowing from Jesus. It means "to cure and make completely whole." As a physician, Luke would not tolerate positive thinking, hype, or phoniness. He is describing the real thing, the power of the Spirit gushing through the Anointed One.

Many years ago, I hosted a young, evangelistic music group. They toured the country performing in various venues and arrived in Massachusetts in their old yellow school bus. They were tired of the bus, so I drove them in my car to shop for their needs. As we rode along, the subject of healing arose.

"Why don't we see healing today as in the time of Christ?" one of the men asked.

The Lord gave me a spontaneous answer, "you need two things to enable healing–the Word that produces faith, and the presence of Jesus."

A quiet peace filled the car as we mulled these words over in our minds.

Do you need healing?

Seek the presence of the Lord. Power comes from him.

Do you need freedom from troubles, worries, compulsiveness, tempting obsessions, or unbearable habits? Jesus heals them all.

Back in our passage above, the disciples watched and learned. Sign up for this list–put your name on the record of disciples–because the extraordinary can happen through you.

Oh God, I want to be one of those disciples who walk with Jesus. I want to see his healing power flowing from me to people in need. There are so many wallowing in the valley of despair and heartache. I want to reach out, touching you, and attach myself to your presence, so your power will flow through me. Make it happen, Lord, for your glory. Amen

Blessings and Woes

Looking at his disciples, he said:

"Blessed are you who are poor, for yours is the kingdom of God.

Blessed are you who hunger now, for you will be satisfied.

Blessed are you who weep now, for you will laugh.

Blessed are you when men hate you, when they exclude you and insult you and reject your name as evil, because of the Son of Man.

"Rejoice in that day and leap for joy, because great is your reward in heaven. For that is how their fathers treated the prophets.

"But woe to you who are rich, for you have already received your comfort.

Woe to you who are well fed now, for you will go hungry.

Woe to you who laugh now, for you will mourn and weep.

Woe to you when all men speak well of you,

for that is how their fathers treated the false prophets. Luke 6:20–26

Descending from the mountaintop of prayer, Christ delivers the "Sermon on the Level." Hungry and hurting people came searching for relief from their pain and hope for their future. Jesus chose twelve Disciples to deliver his message to the masses. Healing, yes. Deliverance, absolutely, but no one expected a sermon that would turn their lives upside down.

One would think that Christ was looking for dynamic leaders to engage the world with his message, or perhaps, with influential and powerful people. But he didn't. Well, how about people who were well-adjusted and happy? No, it is the poor, hungry, hurting, and rejected who are promised blessings.

Paradoxically, the Lord presents three challenges and rebukes. First, "Blessed are the poor...woe to you who are rich." Jesus leaned toward the needy and disenfranchised. The Greek word translated as "poor" literally means "to crouch or kneel in humble dependence." Poverty breeds dependence. God loves those who are dependent on Him. God's affections are for those who run to Him in a child-like fashion.

The second principle in this passage concerns those who hunger. Few people are more desperate than those who don't know where their next meal is coming from. Christ is calling for followers who long for him like a hungry person craves food. They will find fulfillment that satisfies. The lesson of Christian history is that the poor are the most receptive to the gospel, and it changes their lives. Then, they begin to prosper in their work, and their subsequent affluence causes their love for Christ to grow cold. May we heed Christ's warning of the dangers of a full belly. May God keep us hungry for him!

The blessing of sorrow is one that none of us would seek, but inevitably it finds us. Imagine the grief that God experiences as He witnesses the abuse humanity inflicts on each other. The Lord sees the troubled soul. Jesus consoles the hurting heart if we will only turn in faith toward Him. The challenge is to live with God's burden for His distressed children. Beware the lukewarm faith that accompanies this life's comforts and dulls our hearts to the needs of hurting people.

It is not wrong to be prosperous, healthy, and happy, but our hearts must stay soft to the needs of the poor, hurting, and afflicted. No matter our station in life, dependence on God, and trust in His provision is our daily bread.

When I was eleven years old, I lived with my mother and two baby brothers in East Los Angeles. We were on welfare. Life was hard. I had a daily paper route, where I had to collect the money each month from my customers. There were times that my mother would tell me to keep collecting until I had enough tips to buy milk for the babies. I know poverty. Hunger will breed either fear or faith—in me it bred the unconscious fear of never having enough.

Genesis 17 details God's encounter with Abraham as God provides a sacrifice and reveals himself as *El Shaddai*—the *All-Sufficient One*. The root word here, *shad,* means *breast* in Hebrew. This name shows God completely nourishes, satisfies, and supplies his people with provision for all their needs as a mother would her child. The scriptures paint this intimate picture of a nursing mother giving sustenance and security to her infant, so God provides for us.

He loves us. He loves us. He loves us. Intimately, he provides for us and calms our inner fears.

Dear God, it feels so awkward and strange to let you near my heart. I spend my life protecting and hiding my inner thoughts only to find that you were there all the time. Draw me to your heart and allow me to rest there. I hear Christ's call to stay hungry—I hunger for you. I need your sufficiency to fill my emptiness. Protect me from the dangers of becoming lukewarm in my faith. I want to live with a burden for your distressed children. I accept your loving provision even as a child receives from his mother. Amen.

Supernatural Love

"Love your enemies, do good to those who hate you, bless those who curse you, and pray for those who spitefully use you. To him who strikes you on the one cheek, offer the other also. And from him who takes away your cloak, do not with-hold your tunic either. Give to everyone who asks of you. And from him who takes away your goods do not ask them back." Luke 6:27–30, NKJV

The story is told of a missionary returning home after a period of intense ministry on the field. She was looking forward to a time of rest in her apartment. She imagined a time of prayerful reflection, so she gave special attention to cleaning and decorating her outdoor patio for her special place with God. That's when the trouble started.

In her long absence, a young family had moved in next door. They played loud Heavy Metal music late into the night. They screamed obscenities at each other all day. Their children urinated in the yard in broad daylight just outside her patio. Her tranquility departed. Anger took its place. The crisis came when the children discovered a can of orange spray paint. They used it all over her peaceful patio sanctuary. She was livid and cried out to the Lord, "I cannot love them. I hate them."

Recognizing her hatred toward her neighbors was a sin, the woman confessed her need for God's grace. As she did, the scripture came to her, *And beyond all these things put on love, which is the perfect bond of unity* (Colossians 3:14, NASB). So, she chose to wrap herself in the love of God like a coat. The returned missionary made a list of what she would do if she loved her annoying neighbors, then she set about doing those things.

She baked cookies for them and offered to babysit for free. She invited the mother over for coffee, then the most amazing thing happened. She began to understand and have empathy for her newfound friends. The woman saw the horrible pressures the family lived under and truly began to love those who had been her enemies. She gave away kindness without expecting anything in return.

The day came when her neighbors moved away. She wept for them. A supernatural love captured her heart as she journeyed toward the love of God.

Christ commands us to love our enemies and thereby provokes us to walk a pathway of faith. Only through God's help can we possibly love the unlovely or give to those who cannot repay. Doing good to those who hate us is utterly beyond us until we ask the Lord for His help.

Some folks are exasperating. Some people lie and blame us for things that are not our fault. Our feelings naturally grow to despise them. Our dislike for them seems justified. Are there those who have hurt, cursed, or abused us leading us to rationalize our hatred for them? If so, we are in trouble. The love of God is not in us. These feelings can lead to our downfall or our greatest opportunity.

God chose to love us while we were his enemies. We were doomed sinners, and he went the extra mile by sending his son to convey his inexpressible love for us. Peter denied the Lord three times in the hour when Jesus needed him most (John 18:25-27). Yet, Christ looked upon him with love, planned to forgive him, and looked beyond Peter's sin to his God-designed future.

Now we are commanded to do the same. If we ask God to help us, we can draw upon his inexhaustible grace. Love the unlikeable. Forgive the unforgivable. Walk in God's supernatural love.

Dear Lord Jesus, this passage overwhelms me. How can I possibly love the unlovable? Forgive the debt? Forget the insult? I need your help, or I will utterly fail. You are my inexhaustible resource. You are my supply of love. Banish revenge from my heart I pray and dislodge the root of bitterness that has kept me bound all these years. Give me eyes to see beyond the things that offend me and to see irritations as an opportunity to demonstrate your sacrificial love. I pray for the faith to give to all those who ask me even as you forgive me so freely. In your name, I pray. Amen.

The Boomerang Kingdom

Judge not, and you shall not be judged.
Condemn not, and you shall not be condemned.
Forgive, and you will be forgiven. Give and it will
be given to you: good measure, pressed down,
shaken together, and running over will be put into
your bosom. For with the same measure that you
use, it will be measured back to you."

Luke 6:37–38, NKJV

There was a muscleman featured at a state fair, demonstrating feats of strength to the crowd. He broke a board in two with his bare hands. He tore a large phone book in half and squeezed a cup of lemon juice from a lemon. He then turned to the spectators with the lemon in his hand and defied anyone to match his power feats. The strongman offered a day's wage to anyone who could squeeze another drop out of his lemon.

A smallish man in the back of the crowd piped up, "I'll give it a try."

The bald, older man stepped sheepishly to the stage and took the lemon. He quickly squeezed another cup of juice from the fruit as the crowd gasped in surprise. The muscleman, speechless, managed to mumble, "How did you do that?"

"Aw, that ain't nothing," the old man replied, "I'm a deacon down at the local church, and I take the offering each week. I could squeeze blood out of a turnip." Of course, everyone gave a knowing nod.

Ministries across the country use Luke 6:38 each week to encourage their people, "Give and it will be given to you," they say. While this is a reasonable application of the scripture, Jesus says much more. His message conveys the dynamic boomerang effect of the Kingdom of God.

Jesus teaches His disciples how we are to treat people who are outside of the household of faith, "Love your enemies...do good to those who spitefully use you..." He also speaks to his disciples about how to treat each other. To give forgiveness to others multiplies forgiveness back to you.

As a person who frequently needs forgiveness for things I have said or done, I must often sow the seed of forgiveness. There is a mental aspect to Christ's commands. If I think I know a person's motive I have crossed the line and judged them. I have presumptuously sat in God's seat of judgment. I don't belong there.

It is one thing to be upset with another driver on the road. It is another to decide on his mental capacity or the legitimacy of his birth. To judge another's thinking or motive is God's place—not ours. It is prudent to use discernment in making decisions about your actions, but we cannot judge.

Be not deceived my friend, for God is not mocked. Whatever you sow in your mind is what you will reap. What you give away is what will come back to you.

An extended family member who briefly lived with us had a horrible toothache that required extraction. He didn't have a job or dental insurance, so I had to co-sign a form that promised to pay the bill. He vowed to take care of the bill, but I ended up paying the $1,500 debt after he missed many payments. I was justifiably angry, furious actually. I asked Jesus to help me forgive him. True to his word, God helped me. I now have my family member back. I'm free to love him again.

The boomerang effect of the kingdom is working! Jesus redeems adverse circumstances into positive results.

Are you giving a happy, cheerful attitude away to others, one that is free of condemnation of their actions? What are you giving to people around you? Are you thoughtful and considerate of the challenges that others might be facing? Do you know there are reasons people do the things they do? What are you giving to God? Are you trusting God to help you love the unlovable? Are you trusting God to help you to forgive the unforgivable?

Dear Lord, your words seem so impossible. Did you design them that way, so I would have to depend on you to help me? I want to follow in your footsteps. I need the help of the Holy Spirit. When I stand before you, I want to bear the marks of forgiving the unforgivable and the stripes of loving those who have abused me. Strengthen me. I pray in the name of the Father. Amen.

The House That
Jesus Builds

"No good tree bears bad fruit, nor does a bad tree bear good fruit. Each tree is recognized by its own fruit. People do not pick figs from thornbushes, or grapes from briers. The good man brings good things out of the good stored up in his heart, and the evil man brings evil things out of the evil stored up in his heart. For out of the overflow of his heart his mouth speaks.

"Why do you call me, 'Lord, Lord,' and do not do what I say? I will show you what he is like who comes to me and hears my words and puts them into practice. He is like a man building a house, who dug down deep and laid the foundation on rock. When a flood came, the torrent struck that house but could not shake it, because it was well built. But the one who hears my words

and does not put them into practice is like a man who built a house on the ground without a foundation. The moment the torrent struck that house, it collapsed and its destruction was complete. Luke 6:43–49

The boy was five years old when his parents decided they weren't happy with each other. His father left without saying goodbye. His mother raised him, and the adults sought happiness in new places. Heartache germinated in the child until its rotten, wormy fruit was laid bare for all the world to see. Years of anger and loneliness festered into his divorce. Finally, his emotional tumors drove him to a counselors' office. He was fifty years old. I know, because that little boy was me.

Sociologists convey that we are each the composite of our parent's genes and the upbringing that follows. It is fatalistic to say your personality is hostage to genetics and environment, but life experience bears this out. An acorn grows into an oak tree. A pomegranate seed grows into a pomegranate tree. No matter how badly a pomegranate seed might want to be an oak, its fate is determined. Soil and weather influence the development of trees, but their destiny is inevitable. Thankfully, humans are not bound by our sin-tainted physiology. Jesus shows us the way out of that trap.

"Each tree is recognized by its own fruit," Jesus said in Luke 6:43. "People do not pick figs from thornbushes, or grapes from briers. The good man brings good things out of the good stored up in his heart, and the evil man brings evil things out of the evil stored up in his heart". He seems to be saying, "you are who you are."

Fortunately, Christ invokes a vital pivot point. He interjects that life can swivel on what you put into your heart. Store good things in your heart, and good results follow.

The quality and character of our lives hinge on our choices. The master teacher illustrates with the story in Luke's gospel about a house built upon a rock. To lay a building foundation in ancient times, people had to excavate down into the earth with a pick and shovel. They would dig until they reached what excavators call "hardpan," that solid rock surface deep below the topsoil. Without the aid of a backhoe or bulldozer, it was hard work. Many people did not dig deep enough and built their house foundation on sandy soil, inviting eventual disaster as their home washed away. But diligent people would continue to dig until they reached hardpan and constructed their home on solid footing. It was tough work, but their dwelling would last for hundreds of years.

As we choose to obey the Word of God, we are building strength and creating the groundwork of a new destiny. The abundant life will follow as surely as building a house on a good foundation will ensure stability.

Tragically, it is becoming more common to meet people who are confident of God's goodness yet have no idea how to live a Christian life. Recently, Justin Bieber, the current celebrity train-wreck, was arrested for drunk driving and racing his sports car over a hundred miles per hour while intoxicated. He mumbled afterward in slang how he knew that God loved him, and everybody needed to, "just stop all the hatin'."

Yes, God loves Justin, but his house is falling apart due to his behavior.

Personal liberty is not the freedom to do as we please. Many live as if happiness is the goal in life. I submit that your character is the substance of life. That is a quality sometimes hard to define. "Character is like a tree and reputation like a shadow," said Abraham Lincoln. "The shadow is what we think of it; the tree is the real thing."

Christ rebuilt my life and character as he taught me how to receive Father God's love. Where my parents failed, the Lord succeeded. The dangers of sin and corruption still knock at the door, but if I embrace God's truth, I have a shield of protection. God is transforming the hurting little boy I once was.

God's Word is to our soul what protein is to the body. It builds muscle strength. Take the story of the house built on rock and think about it. Chew it. Swallow it. Let it form a strong character in you. Build your life on the words of Jesus. Let them bear healthy fruit in you.

Father God, you can accomplish what an army of counselors can never do. Help me to be a person who will bear good fruit. Give me the faith to stand amid life's storms. Build in me the foundation upon which you can construct a house that will endure with strength and character. Amen.

God Consciousness

When Jesus had finished saying all this in the hearing of the people, he entered Capernaum. There a centurion's servant, whom his master valued highly, was sick and about to die. The centurion heard of Jesus and sent some elders of the Jews to him, asking him to come and heal his servant. When they came to Jesus, they pleaded earnestly with him, "This man deserves to have you do this, because he loves our nation and has built our synagogue." So Jesus went with them.

He was not far from the house when the centurion sent friends to say to him: "Lord, don't trouble yourself, for I do not deserve to have you come under my roof. That is why I did not even consider myself worthy to come to you. But say the word, and my servant will be healed. For I myself am a man under authority, with soldiers under me. I tell this one, 'Go,' and he goes; and that one, 'Come,' and he comes. I say to my servant, 'Do this,' and he does it."

When Jesus heard this, he was amazed at him, and turning to the crowd following him, he said, "I tell you, I have not found such great faith even in Israel." Then the men who had been sent returned to the house and found the servant well.
Luke 7:1–10

There is nothing more important in the Christian life than to *know* Jesus. Having faith and the consciousness of the Lord in our daily affairs generates a spiritual dynamic that is unstoppable. Our failures and successes hinge on this one truth—do we know God's direction in the matter?

Jesus is at the beginning of His journey as he passes through Capernaum to His next assignment in ministry when he is interrupted. Some Jewish Elders plead that He comes to a Roman Centurion home to heal a dying servant. The Elders commend the Centurion. Luke7:4,5 states they "pleaded" with Jesus, "This man deserves to have you do this because he loves our nation and has built our synagogue."

The perspective of the Elders is flawed. They viewed the Centurion on external qualities, "he built us a synagogue," rather than internal qualities such as faith and godliness.

Psalm 53:1–3 and Romans 3:10 state that there is "none righteous, no not one." We cannot come to God based on our own good works as our righteousness is as filthy rags before God.

The Centurion shows us a better way! A centurion was a battle-proven officer in the army of ancient Rome. Centurions got their name because they commanded 100 men (*Centuria* means 100 in Latin). They were often highly respected, sometimes greatly feared, and considered the backbone of the Roman Army. Typically, the Romans viewed the Jews as dirt beneath their feet. Yet, this Roman sends a message to Jesus, "I am not worthy that you should enter under my roof...but say the word, and my servant will be healed," Luke 7:7, NKJV. This man is humble enough to see his unworthiness in the light of Christ's majesty. He is aware of who Jesus is in person and insightful enough to be conscious of God's Presence in Christ.

Humility is not to think of oneself as a slimy worm. But instead, to view yourself in the light of Christ's glory before whom we should declare like the Elders in Revelation 4:11, NKJV, "You are worthy, O Lord, to receive glory and honor and power."

The Centurion describes how he came to understand faith and humility. He was both a man under submission to his superiors, and he had command of people under himself. A Centurian gives orders and knows they are followed. He understood that Christ could "send the word," and God's work would be done. True faith is the confidence and consciousness of the God who is already at work.

Luke 7:9 says that Jesus "marveled" at the Centurion's faith. There are only two times in the Scriptures that Jesus marvels, or is amazed, here and when he ministered in His hometown of Nazareth. Christ marveled at their unbelief. In one instance, Jesus is amazed by a person's faith. In another, He marvels at their lack of faith. Where do you fall in this spectrum of faith?

The beauty here lies where the Centurion exercised his faith on behalf of someone else rather than his own needs or wants. The servant of this man lies desperately ill until his master sends a message to Jesus. The Centurion had empathy for his servant's suffering. He coupled that empathy with an understanding of Christ's ability to alleviate that sickness. Have you ever noticed that you have a higher percentage of answers to your prayers when you pray for others rather than yourself?

When Christ looks upon us at which will He marvel? Who around you are suffering? Can you exercise your faith way on behalf of someone else? Are you conscious of a God-reality at work? Are you humble enough to yield to God's control?

Oh Lord, so many questions flood my mind from this passage! I want to have the faith of this Centurion. Please help me to stop thinking about myself all the time. Enable me to feel the pain of others before I dwell on my own problems. You are the object of my faith, and you are the answer to my prayers. In your name, I pray. Amen.

A Tale of Two Crowds

Now it happened, the day after, that He went into a city called Nain; and many of His disciples went with Him, and a large crowd. And when He came near the gate of the city, behold, a dead man was being carried out, the only son of his mother; and she was a widow. And a large crowd from the city was with her.

When the Lord saw her, his heart went out to her and he said, "Don't cry."

Then he went up and touched the coffin, and those carrying it stood still. He said, "Young man, I say to you, get up!" The dead man sat up and began to talk, and Jesus gave him back to his mother.

They were all filled with awe and praised God. "A great prophet has appeared among us," they said. "God has come to help his people." This news about Jesus spread throughout Judea and the surrounding country. Luke 7:11–17

Jesus never went to a funeral that He didn't interrupt with a resurrection. Dead people getting up at funerals can get uncomfortable. The biblical story of Christ raising the widow's son from the dead in Luke 7:11-17 presents us with certain contradictions. It insults our twenty-first-century mindset concerning death and life.

Jesus came straight away from His great sermon in Capernaum, followed by healing the Centurion's servant. Consequently, a great crowd followed Him to His next destination–the village of Nain. Resting about nine miles south of Nazareth, Nain was the site of several miracles during Christ's ministry. As Christ's victory parade approaches the village, they encounter a wailing crowd coming out of Nain. The mourners surround the funeral bier of a dead man, the son of a widow. The dissimilarity of life and death, joy and despair could not have been more profound.

The story's hinge point turns as Christ sees the weeping, distraught mother and has compassion for her. Christ's sympathy steals the show. He feels her pain and bears her sorrow. Contrast that to the paid grievers carrying the coffin and body.

Hebrews 4:15 says that our Lord is "touched with the feelings of our infirmities." His compassion is unswerving even in the face of death, *especially* in the face of death. Jesus, moved by compassion, tells the woman, "Do not weep."

The group following Jesus and the crowd of mourners formed a standoff when the Author of Life steps forward and touches the coffin, clearly violating Jewish law. Jews were forbidden to touch a dead person as they would be considered ceremonially unclean. The two crowds gasp at Christ's audacity. The Master's touch goes where others do not want to go, even into a dead man's coffin. He spoke, and the world changed, "Young man, I say to you, arise" (Luke 7:14 NKJV.) Life confronted death. The young man rose and spoke. Astonishment seized the crowd as they witnessed resurrection life in action.

But we still live under the shadow of Death. Most of us have not seen resurrections at funerals. This question of faith slaps us in the face when the scriptures speak to us in 1 Peter 1:7-9, (NKJV) "...at the revelation of Jesus Christ, who having not seen you love. Though now you do not see Him, yet believing, you rejoice with joy inexpressible and full of glory, receiving the end of your faith—the salvation of your souls." Though we do not see resurrection now with our natural eyes, an eternal quality of life is our present joy and our future destiny.

There is one more paradox in our passage. Jesus was a living "only Son" destined to die on a cruel rugged cross while the young, dead "only son" was on his way to encounter resurrection life. Two "only sons" meet at the intersection of life and death. Life was given to that young man at Nain because he met Jesus and because Christ was willing to die for him. Ephesians 2:4-5 (NKJV) says, "But God, who is rich in mercy, because of His great love with which He loved us, even when we were dead in trespasses, made us alive together with Christ." To all who have faith in Christ, meet life!

Maker of heaven and earth, I come asking you to breathe into me the breath of life once again. My life is decaying, and I need your fresh touch of life. I am on my way to my funeral, for surely death comes for all mortal people. Come to my funeral Lord and lift me in the great resurrection so I can be with you. I believe you are the resurrection and the life. You are the author, sustainer, and re-creator of the universe. Thank you, Jesus, for dying that I might have life. In your name, I pray. Amen.

Doubt in the Darkness

John's disciples told him about all these things. Calling two of them, he sent them to the Lord to ask, "Are you the one who was to come, or should we expect someone else?"

When the men came to Jesus, they said, "John the Baptist sent us to you to ask, 'Are you the one who was to come, or should we expect someone else?'"

At that very time Jesus cured many who had diseases, sicknesses and evil spirits, and gave sight to many who were blind. So he replied to the messengers, "Go back and report to John what you have seen and heard: The blind receive sight, the lame walk, those who have leprosy are cured, the deaf hear, the dead are raised, and the good news is preached to the poor. Blessed is the man who does not fall away on account of me." Luke 7:18–23

And tell him, 'God blesses those who are not offended by me." Luke 7:23, (NLT)

In the depths of the dungeon, in the very last cell, was a rugged man who was more wild than tame. Breathing holy fire, he had preached the truth to the multitudes and confronted kings with righteous indignation. John the Baptist was a man like no other, yet as the darkness in the dungeon drew longer, his doubts grew crusty like moldy bread. Luke 7:18-36 demonstrates that doubt is a part of the human condition. More importantly, it shows how the Lord responds to our weakness.

John lived free as a desert nomad—before his imprisonment. The sun was his companion by day and the stars his consolation by night. Raging in his bones was the message of God, pointing people toward righteousness. But you don't confront cruel kings like Herod without consequences. So, as the gospel reports, he lands in prison.

Eventually, the news of Jesus' miracles reached the ears of John the Baptist in jail. Herod imprisoned John the Baptist in the palace of Macherus, according to the Jewish historian Flavius Josephus (Antiquities of the Jews, XVIII, V, 2.) The Romans built the facility in 90 AD. John was in prison for over a year when his doubts became overwhelming.

John's messengers to Christ conveyed his question, "Are you the Messiah we've been expecting, or should we keep looking for someone else?" (Luke 7:19, NLT)

John had heard of the miracles Christ performed and the good news He preached. His expectation of a conquering Messiah probably had been brewing in his heart. He must have been saying to himself, "What about me, Jesus, why am I stuck?" He was a man just like us, and his circumstances were undermining his faith. This challenge comes to everyone who tries to walk by faith in God. It is the moment when you decide if you will trust the Lord no matter what.

Christ's answer to John is the same as it is to us. Remember what Jesus has done, the miracles He has worked, and the salvation He has provided.

"Go back to John and tell him what you have seen and heard—the blind see, the lame walk, the lepers are cured, deaf people hear, the dead are raised to life, and the Good News is being preached to the poor." Jesus concludes his message with a curious, seemingly insignificant tag line, "And tell him, 'God blesses those who are not offended by me." (Luke 7:22–23 NLT)

The Greek word the Scriptures used here for "offended" is "skandalizoo," which means "a stumbling block, or to bait a trap." Jesus is saying, *Don't fall into the trap of doubt because you are going through difficult circumstances right now. Don't stumble because you hear of me doing great things in others while you feel trapped. Hold steady in the storm.*

Christ did not rebuke John the Baptist for his unbelief. Instead, He gives him the highest commendation, "I tell you, of all who have ever lived, none is greater than John. Yet even the most insignificant person in the Kingdom of God is greater than he is!" (Luke 7:28, NLT) While Jesus praises John, he also elevates us.

John was a great prophet, but he was part of the Old Testament economy. You are a believer in the saving Christ. John was a herald of the King. You are now a child of the Highest God. John was a friend of the Bridegroom, but you are the Bride. The light of God has risen upon you. Banish doubt and darkness in Jesus' name!

Lord, I admit I have my times of doubt. I choose to believe in you because you are my hope for a better life. Thank you I am not trapped in a dungeon cell like John the Baptist. Sometimes I feel imprisoned in my thoughts and habits. You are the miracle worker, and I need you to set me free today. I want to worship you without inhibition or constraint. I pray this in Christ's name. Amen.

The Greatest of All

After John's messengers left, Jesus began to speak to the crowd about John: "What did you go out into the desert to see? A reed swayed by the wind? If not, what did you go out to see? A man dressed in fine clothes? No, those who wear expensive clothes and indulge in luxury are in palaces. But what did you go out to see? A prophet? Yes, I tell you, and more than a prophet. This is the one about whom it is written:

> *"'I will send my messenger ahead of you,*
>
> *who will prepare your way before you.'*

I tell you, among those born of women there is no one greater than John; yet the one who

is least in the kingdom of God is greater than he."
Luke 7:24–28

He came to the door just as I was closing the bookstore and coffee shop. "Can I come into the coffee shop and get a latte?"

My friend, Bill, had just come from church and was glowing with enthusiasm as he stepped in and submitted his order. I'm sure the other employees were not happy I delayed our closing. Unconcerned with their dismay and overflowing with the presence of God, Bill began to share with the workers about the wonderful blessings of God. They were captivated by his words and showed genuine interest.

My friend was God's messenger that night. His witness will reverberate through eternity. That night Bill stood beside John the Baptist and pointed the way to God's son. In that, he was the greatest.

What was it that made John the Baptist "more than a prophet," and caused Christ to say, "there is no one greater than John?" Moses split the Red Sea and carried the commandments down from the mountain. Elijah called down fire from heaven. Elisha raised the dead. Is John greater than them? Yes, and so many more. He pointed people to Jesus, the Messiah.

Certain unique qualities formed the foundation of John's life. First, he was fearless in declaring God's righteousness. God is good and gracious in all his ways, but he is also just. He will judge both the living and the dead. John the Baptist called the king out for marrying his brother's wife. It cost him his head.

John commanded the religious to repent and the wayward to get baptized. He was a fire-breathing man of God who did not compromise with hypocrisy.

John's habit of life also did not allow him to indulge his flesh with comforts and luxury. Not that these are necessarily wrong, but they are counterproductive to living a life of greatness. Any person who aspires to excellence understands that sacrifices are required. An athlete expends his energy daily in developing their skills. A young musician chooses to practice their instrument while the other kids are outside playing. A scholar lives a life of study and seclusion in musty libraries to rise to the top of their discipline.

John the Baptist sought God in the wilds of the desert, and God spoke to him through the wind, the heat, and the silence. He was single-minded in his devotion to the Lord. John was a great prophet because he spoke God's word pointing people to the Messiah.

Living like John the Baptist in today's world seems impossible. Yet, it is the last phrase in Christ's words on the Baptizer that are the most astonishing, "the one who is least in the kingdom of God is greater than he."

Wait. What? How can that be?

In fifty years as a Christian and eight years in Bible College and Seminary, I have never heard this preached or taught. The believer in Jesus is more significant than John the Baptist! You are greater than the prophets? All of them?

Moses and the whole bunch long for what you have. The resurrected Savior lives in you by the power of the Holy Spirit.

So, what is Jesus saying to us in this passage? Point people to the Messiah at all costs. That's what John the Baptist did. Don't let the comforts of the flesh lull you into sleepy, lukewarm Christianity. Embrace the abiding presence of Christ by living in the awareness that the same Spirit who was in John and Jesus is in you.

Bill came to the door of our bookshop café with Jesus overflowing his heart, and he poured liquid love over us. We are called to do the same. The challenge for us is to live with John the Baptist's integrity and forthrightness while pointing people to Jesus. May God empower us all.

Dear Lord, I want to be great like John the Baptist. I ask for your love to overflow my heart and my flesh that I might share the message of salvation through faith in your death, burial, and resurrection. Help me to avoid compromises that reflect poorly on you. Give me the grace and integrity to live entirely for you and with you. In your name, I pray. Amen.

The Great Divide

All the people, even the tax collectors, when they heard Jesus' words, acknowledged that God's way was right, because they had been baptized by John. But the Pharisees and experts in the law rejected God's purpose for themselves, because they had not been baptized by John.

"To what, then, can I compare the people of this generation? What are they like? They are like children sitting in the marketplace and calling out to each other:

"'We played the flute for you, and you did not dance; we sang a dirge, and you did not cry.'

> *For John the Baptist came neither eating bread nor drinking wine, and you say, 'He has a demon.' The Son of Man came eating and drinking, and you say, 'Here is a glutton and a drunkard, a friend of tax collectors and "sinners." ' But wisdom is proved right by all her children."*
> Luke 7:29–35

"You're full of it," my best friend spits out the words.

"You want to fight about it?" I said, waving my eight-year-old fist at him. "I'll give you a knuckle sandwich,"

"Hey, what is 'it' anyway?" he said, bringing our Three Stooges comic routine to an end.

Argument and controversy seem to plague every generation. Many times, we are like the people in this passage. We fight about who is right, and we miss the fact Jesus is with us. The division we have created becomes a stumbling block to our faith.

Luke shows us two types of people. First, those baptized by John the Baptist, who acknowledged that God's ways are right. In contrast, the Pharisees and experts in the law rejected John's message and refused baptism.

John the Baptist lived a sacrificial life, depriving himself of the comforts of typical food, regular clothing, and even housing, in his quest to draw closer to God. His message called the people to repent and turn back to God (Luke 3:38).

The scribes and the Pharisees criticized him for his austere lifestyle and rejected his message. Jesus lived his life among people–eating and drinking with them, attending weddings, and celebrating life while preaching, "Repent for the kingdom of God is at hand" (Matthew 4:17). The religious types criticized him as a carouser and drinker. This same judgmental spirit often undermines the work of Christ in the world today.

Beneath the criticism was the apparent fact that the critics did not want to change their ways, so they deflected and slammed the messengers. Both John and Christ were calling people to change their lives and turn back to God with their whole heart.

Neither John nor Jesus would allow criticism to deter them from sharing God's message.

What is in your heart?

What would God say to you?

Your heart is a vessel full of your thoughts, feelings, and a host of opinions. Will we allow criticism, selfishness, and defensiveness to dominate our consciousness?

Our mind usually responds to the world, "What's in it for me?" God seeks to lift us from the morass of our muddled thinking into clarity. When confronted with the realities of God's truth, people will choose to respond in faith or criticize in unbelief.

Jesus concludes his teaching with the phrase, "wisdom is proved right by all her children" (v.35). The word translated here as "wisdom" comes from the Greek term *Sophia*, meaning "knowledge of how to regulate one's relationship with God; this wisdom is related to goodness." John and Jesus, for all their differences, represent wisdom. John's fiery preaching was so different from the kindness and gentleness Jesus personified. Yet, they both had a relationship with God that produced children for God. God's wisdom in each of them is justified by those who choose to become his children.

People may argue over theological tenets that only result in division. Many may argue over whose lifestyle is godlier. Similar to the people in Christ's day, we have created our great divide. But we all sound like just another *Three Stooges* act when we do. The only children we reproduce are born out of pride, strife, and self-righteousness. God forbid!

We demonstrate wisdom when we choose to respond to the goodness God extends to us through his son Jesus. People may misuse their freewill to frustrate God's purposes, and they may be deaf to God's appeal. But God chose the dangerous way of love to communicate with us. James 2:13 says, "Mercy triumphs over judgment." No coercion, no law, and no mandate will fulfill his purpose, only the loving call to come to the Savior Jesus. In the end, love will prevail and bring forth children who will shine like the noon-day sun.

Dear Father, help me take my eyes off life's external qualities and put them squarely on Jesus, your son. Help me not to be defensive, deflecting from your message to me. I choose to hear and obey you. I want to love like you loved and live as you lived. Open my ears to listen to your message to me today and empower me to respond in faith. I pray in Christ's name. Amen.

The Anointed Gift

When a woman who had lived a sinful life in that town learned that Jesus was eating at the Pharisee's house, she brought an alabaster jar of perfume, and as she stood behind him at his feet weeping, she began to wet his feet with her tears. Then she wiped them with her hair, kissed them and poured perfume on them." Luke 7:37–38

Recently I asked my twelve-year-old grandson, Lucas, what he wanted for his birthday. He pondered deeply for a moment then responded, "Oh, just a wad of cash."

While any self-respecting adolescent would welcome money, everything in me revolted at the notion of a cash gift. I had to ask myself, "Why not just give cash and skip the whole shopping hassle?" No amount of money could ever convey my heart for my loved ones. Really, what is a present without love?

The power of a gift given with a heart-load of love becomes the occasion for a compelling message from Christ in Luke 7:36–50. "A woman who had led a sinful life" is the central figure in the drama. The story could just as easily be about you or me. We are sinful people. The woman shows us what forgiveness does to a person. It wrecks your outer facade and breaks open emotions you never thought you could display. This nameless person demonstrates the impact of unashamed, uncompromising, and unadulterated affection lavished on a Savior who forgives to the utmost. She bathed Christ's feet with her tears because he washed away her sins.

The woman's behavior in this passage conveys immense gratitude. Broken by the events of her life, Jesus somehow mends her back together. Unreserved forgiveness evokes unrestrained worship. Though the people present were indignant at the raw display of her feelings, she doesn't care what they think. She doesn't allow people to spoil the intensity of her expression. Her life was a trail of tears that led her to Jesus. Her tears wet the Savior's feet, and she wiped them with her hair. She pours oil upon Christ's feet as she poured her life out as an offering.

As the unnamed lady wept and wiped Christ's feet with her hair, cleansing tears of repentance flowed. The Pharisee thought Jesus should have known how bad a woman this was kissing His feet. Yet, Jesus saw the depth of her devotion. Indeed, those who are forgiven much love much. Brokenness is more attractive to God than our pious pride.

The present awareness of our sin should no longer make us feel guilty but rather drive us to Christ's feet with the sacrificial gift of our devotion. Is it pride or fear that hinders us from displaying this kind of thankfulness?

Our transgressions have been washed away in the cleansing tide of Christ's great love. Author John Bevere says in his book, *Bait of Satan,* "A person who cannot forgive has forgotten how great a debt God has forgiven them."

Nelson Mandela passed away in 2013, and the world poured out their affection in his memory. He deserves his place in history as one of our time's great leaders, primarily because of his ability to be gracious. Mandela forgave his captors even after twenty-seven years of cruel imprisonment. Beyond that, he led his people to reconciliation, saying, "Forgiveness liberates the soul. That is why it is such a powerful weapon."

Jesus came with the express purpose of forgiving sinful people. His intended purpose was to go to the cross and die for us so that God could justly forgive us. Radical worship is the only reasonable response to so profound a sacrifice. The revelation of God's gracious forgiveness and generous acceptance is a mystery we will continue to explore for eternity. I ask today how many love Jesus to the point of tears? How many love Christ enough to kiss the Savior's feet with pure-hearted worship? Who will anoint the Messiah's feet with the gift of anointed gratitude?

O God, break my heart open that I might worship like this woman. Humble me that I can feel the depth of emotion and gratitude that she demonstrates. I bow before you to honor and worship you with all my heart. Thank you for the gift of your son. Remove the scars and the guilt that hinder me from pouring out this kind of feeling upon you. You are worthy of my praise and adoration. In Christ's name, I pray, amen.

Who Will Weep?

When the Pharisee who had invited him saw this, he said to himself, "If this man were a prophet, he would know who is touching him and what kind of woman she is — that she is a sinner."

Jesus answered him, "Simon, I have something to tell you."

"Tell me, teacher," he said.

"Two men owed money to a certain moneylender. One owed him five hundred denarii, and the other fifty. Neither of them had the money to pay him back, so he canceled the debts of both. Now which of them will love him more?"

Simon replied, "I suppose the one who had the bigger debt canceled."

"You have judged correctly," Jesus said.

Then he turned toward the woman and said to Simon, "Do you see this woman? I came into your house. You did not give me any water for my feet, but she wet my feet with her tears and wiped them with her hair. You did not give me a kiss, but this woman, from the time I entered, has not stopped kissing my feet. You did not put oil on my head, but she has poured perfume on my feet. Therefore, I tell you, her many sins have been for-given — for she loved much. But he who has been forgiven little loves little."

Then Jesus said to her, "Your sins are for-given."

The other guests began to say among themselves, "Who is this who even forgives sins?"

Jesus said to the woman, "Your faith has saved you; go in peace." Luke 7:39–50

My friends introduced me to the Lord as a teenager in 1970, during the height of the Jesus Movement. In those days, altar calls were common in churches, and sinners would come forward to confess the prayer of faith. In the heat of the moment, people would often cry tears of repentance and express other emotions. When I went forward, I prayed the prayer and felt nothing. I knew I had decided to follow Christ and was now a Christian, but I was un-moved on an emotional level.

Well, I'm a man, and men don't show feelings, I rationalized. *I should not base my faith on emotions, anyways.* Yet, I knew I was missing out on a crucial component of spirituality and humanity. Luke brings this element of our faith front and center in today's passage.

The contrast between the weeping woman and Simon, the Pharisee standing aloof, could hardly be more severe. Great tears of repentance and worship rolled off her face as she knelt at Christ's feet. Meanwhile, the Pharisee doesn't offer Jesus a sim-ple courtesy. He seems to say, *who is this semi-fa-mous young rabbi anyway?*

The judgment of the Pharisee weighs in heavily against Christ as he thinks, "If this man were a prophet, he would know who is touching him and what kind of woman she is—that she is a sinner," Luke 7:39.

Jesus responds with a parable to pour grace over the awkward situation. Christ tells of two peo-ple who each owed a debt they could not repay. One had enormous debt, and the other had a small debt. Both receive forgiveness. To the question concerning who would love the forgiver more, the Pharisee logically answers, "I suppose the one who had the bigger debt canceled," Luke 7:43. Jesus commends him for his correct answer and then ap-plies it to the woman and Simon.

Simon neglected to give Jesus the respect due to a household guest. Compare that to the adoration the woman showered upon Christ. She felt remorse for her sins and gratitude toward God's messenger. The Pharisee held back in icy evaluation, judging whether Jesus met his standard for a man of God. The woman knew her need for forgiveness. The Pharisee knew the letter of scriptures but was ignorant concerning the state of his soul.

Proverbs 21:4 (TPT) speaks to Simon and many religious people of our day, "Arrogance, superiority, and pride are the fruits of wickedness and the true definition of sin."

People too often compare themselves to others to lift themselves in their own estimation. That age-old trap snared Simon. Once entangled, he feels justified in judging the woman caught for her past sin. Man's judgment kills, while mercy makes room for forgiveness.

Many years ago, divorce brought me to my lowest point. Failure and guilt dripped off the edges of my life. Yet, God came so near to me, like he was always in the room with me and my pain.

While God's forgiveness was instant, grief haunted me. At fifty years of age, I finally turned to a counselor who taught me to grieve my life losses. The therapist encouraged me to journal my thoughts regarding my losses and then cry for fifteen minutes. I thought she must be crazier than me.

Since I paid the counselor for her advice, I felt I should at least try her medicine. For three days, I journaled each morning and cried genuine tears. Then it happened. I was suddenly set free. It was as if a thick, spaghetti-like ball of rotted emotion in my chest dissolved. I could breathe deeply once more.

The stranglehold on my emotions was released, and I could *feel* again. Grief dissipated, and the tears dried up. I discovered a new-found ability to express appropriate feelings.

I found the joy of gratitude and worship. I joined the ranks of people who, like the weeping woman in our passage, love Jesus for the forgiveness and freedom he gives.

Were it not for the grace of God setting me free I would have died a cold, lonely person. By the mercy of God, I can weep tears of gratitude and joy.

My God, my Savior, and my Lord, thank you for your presence and the grace you shower upon sinners—of whom I am chief. I repent of the times in my life when I looked down upon others in judgment and pride. Love and compassion are so much better. I choose to bow at your feet and adore you—the king of mercy. In your name, I pray. Amen.

The Kind of People Who Walk with Jesus

After this, Jesus traveled about from one town and village to another, proclaiming the good news of the kingdom of God. The Twelve were with him, and also some women who had been cured of evil spirits and diseases: Mary (called Magdalene) from whom seven demons had come out; Joanna the wife of Cuza, the manager of Herod's household; Susanna; and many others. These women were helping to support them out of their own means. Luke 8:1–3

Christ bursts the barriers of his home region in Galilee and takes his ministry on the road. Villages and towns need to hear his wonderful news and witness his mighty power. Out of the synagogues, he plunges into the masses. He brings this curious group of followers with him—disciples, the dispossessed, the needy, the influential, even women.

The Gospel of Luke is unique in the emphasis it puts upon the activity of women involved with Christ's ministry. Some would say that Luke has a pro-woman agenda. I believe that as a non-Jew, he sees the tremendous contributions women make to the preaching of the gospel.

One could see how taking women with you on the road could be problematic. How does that even work while walking town to town, sometimes sleeping by the side of the road? We don't know. We do know that Jesus made it work without any hint of impropriety.

Beyond the twelve disciples, we see there were people following Jesus who were healed and delivered of demons. These people gave testimony to Christ as living evidence of his miracle-working power. People tend to think of demon-possessed people as mentally ill. Whatever it was, Jesus dealt with it and set people free.

Luke introduces us to Mary, called Magdalene. She had seven demons cast out. We can assume when Jesus found her she was a hot mess. We can deduce that Mary was full of all kinds of sin, sickness, and problems. As sick as she was, it is startling to see the transformation in her life.

Mary Magdalene walks with Jesus and is utterly devoted to him. Matthew 27:55 says she followed Jesus from the early days of his ministry in Galilee. Luke shows us here that she walks with Jesus in the middle part of his life. It is at the end of Christ's life that we find Mary most tenacious. She was at his feet during the crucifixion, the first to the tomb following his burial, and she was the first to proclaim his resurrection. Mary hurried to the Disciples to declare the good news to the depressed men. This lady shined as a hero that the early Church would later call "an Apostle to the Apostles."

Luke moves on in his list of faithful women to Joanna, the wife of Cuza. She is an influential staff member of Herod Antipas, the Roman-appointed ruler of Galilee. Herod's palace was in Tiberias, nineteen miles from Nazareth, where Christ grew up. She knew Jesus and was committed to his mission. Joanna remained devoted to Jesus until the end. She traveled with Him on His final journey from Galilee to Jerusalem. She was present at Christ's crucifixion and burial. According to Luke 24:55-56, Joanna returned with the women to anoint his dead body. Later, upon discovering the empty tomb, Joanna and the others ran to report the news to the Apostles.

By welcoming women like Joanna into His inner circle, Jesus broke with Jewish tradition. Social norms did not allow married women to travel with single men. Joanna stepped down from her high social position as a member of Herod Antipas' royal court when she chose to walk with Jesus. Joanna's life is an example of how the gospel demolishes class barriers and social prejudices.

Susanna is also named in this passage but is unknown. She personifies the truth that not only the infamous and notables are followers of the Lord, but also ordinary people. Christ's disciples are certainly a diverse group that includes all kinds of people.

I want to be counted in that group of disciples.

The people who follow Jesus contribute to his ministry from their resources.

Grateful people give.

In 1994, the church that I pastored in Brockton, Massachusetts, built a beautiful, new facility. We encountered expensive setbacks that sapped our energy and our resources. The Lord led me to challenge our church to give a "Harvest Offering." My wife and I wanted to teach our four children to be givers. We withdrew the last of our personal money and got four stacks of one hundred dollar bills. Each of the kids got a pile of cash to give on the altar that "Harvest Sunday."

Our fifteen-year-old daughter, Jessica, led the way. As she approached the altar, she spontaneously looked up and threw the dollar bills high into the air with glee. I was shocked, and the congregation gasped. It was as if the air was sucked out of the room. Then the other children quickly followed her lead. Money flew around the altar. Something in the spirit realm broke in those moments. Joy erupted.

The children's faith set us free from the financial pressure that sapped the energy from our hearts. The total amount of money given that day paled compared to the freedom and faith loosed in the Spirit. Giving sets you free, and the people who walk with Jesus give freely. Just like in our passage today, it was a female who led the way. Christ uses all kinds of people.

Lord Jesus, I want to walk with you every day. I ask you to set me free that I might support your work from my resources. I want to follow you whole-heartedly, not holding anything back from you and your mission to save people. I pray this in your name. Amen.

Christian Dirt

While a large crowd was gathering and people were coming to Jesus from town after town, he told this parable: "A farmer went out to sow his seed. As he was scattering the seed, some fell along the path; it was trampled on, and the birds of the air ate it up. Some fell on rock, and when it came up, the plants withered because they had no moisture. Other seed fell among thorns, which grew up with it and choked the plants. Still other seed fell on good soil. It came up and yielded a crop, a hundred times more than was sown."

When he said this, he called out, "He who has ears to hear, let him hear."

His disciples asked him what this parable meant. He said, "The knowledge of the secrets of the kingdom of God has been given to you, but to others I speak in parables, so that,

"'though seeing, they may not see; though hearing, they may not understand.'

"This is the meaning of the parable: The seed is the word of God. Those along the path are the ones who hear, and then the devil comes and takes away the word from their hearts, so that they may not believe and be saved. Those on the rock are the ones who receive the word with joy when they hear it, but they have no root. They believe for a while, but in the time of testing they fall away. The seed that fell among thorns stands for those who hear, but as they go on their way they are choked by life's worries, riches and pleasures, and they do not mature. But the seed on good soil stands for those with a noble and good heart, who hear the word, retain it, and by persevering produce a crop. Luke 8:4–15

The sign at the state line says, "Nebraska, the Good Life." I testify the expression is valid. The lifestyle is wonderful. From the terrible traffic in troubled Los Angeles to the crazy crowds in New York, the world is a suffocating place. But in Nebraska's fertile soil, people have the quiet confidence that with hard work, things grow.

The Bible says we're descendants of the first man, Adam. The literal rendering of his name means "red earth." God formed humanity when he shaped the dirt and blew in the breath of life. Humans are red clay stuck on ourselves. Jesus explains this dirt phenomenon with a parable about a farmer sowing seed onto various types of soil.

Do we assume we are good soil?

Jesus first speaks of the hardened pathway where daily traffic tramples the seeds. Burnout is the enemy of a thriving faith, and repetitious routine is its evil cousin. Churches exhaust people with too many programs. Liturgies and bulletins all sound the same after a while. Jesus infers something entirely different.

Christ appears to make it difficult for people to understand his message—only those who, "with a noble and good heart," could hear him (v. 15). In *Crazy Love*, Francis Chan suggests Jesus isn't interested in those who fake their discipleship. This discussion begs the question—what kind of dirt are you?

The rocky ground produces a show of faith, but it doesn't last. Our easy-going lifestyle does not serve us well for spirituality. It makes us passive. "It is not scientific doubt, not atheism, not pantheism, not agnosticism, that in our day and in this land is likely to quench the light of the gospel," Frederick Huntington said in 1890. "It is the proud, selfish, luxurious, church-going, hollow-hearted prosperity."

Beware the danger of the good life!

The "thorny soil" shows us how distractions suffocate our confidence in God. Faith cannot grow when we have too much competition crowding our commitment.

"Too much of the good life ends up being toxic, as busyness deforms us spiritually," David Goetz writes in *Death by Suburb*. What are the first things we think of when we wake up, and the last thing we think about when we go to bed? Do we consider our daily priorities more than our love for God and his people?

Do we stifle our trust in God with thoughts like, "I believe in the big guy upstairs," but are too afraid to speak of Jesus out loud?

People starve their faith by only occasionally attending church in between their other activities. Bible study and fellowship produce nutrient-rich soil and feed the seed's transforming power to change their life.

What is the good ground? The heart that is fertile soil is hungry to receive the Word of God. Beyond that, it gives the seed what it needs—room to grow. Time and attention are the precious minerals of good earth. The seed devotes itself to the dirt, and the soil receives it.

The story of the sower and the seed is about the condition of our hearts. What kind of attention and time are we giving to the good seed of Christ planted in us? What type of fruit do we see emerging in our lives? Are our hearts good soil?

O Lord, sometimes I feel like downtrodden soil—walked on and hardened. Help me break up my hardened ground.

Yes, I had times when I received your word joyfully yet allowed the temptations of the world to steal it away. Guilty, I need your grace, Lord. Holy Spirit, cause my roots to grow strong. In your name, I pray. Amen.

Leave the Light On

"No one lights a lamp and hides it in a jar or puts it under a bed. Instead, he puts it on a stand, so that those who come in can see the light. For there is nothing hidden that will not be disclosed, and nothing concealed that will not be known or brought out into the open. Therefore consider carefully how you listen. Whoever has will be given more; whoever does not have, even what he thinks he has will be taken from him. Luke 8:1, 16–18

As my children navigated the minefield of adolescence, one of my jobs was to establish curfews. I always left the front porch and living room lights on until everybody was safely home. Frankly, I couldn't sleep until my kids were home because it's a dark and dangerous world out there.

Transport yourself back to ancient Palestine. You live in a home built with baked brick white-washed by lime. The sleeping areas are in the back or on the roof. You probably have an outer court-yard where visitors pass through to knock at the door. If there is no light of welcome, they will not visit. Jesus tells us to keep our light on so people can find their way to the household of faith.

In our parable today, Christ gives us this great metaphor comparing the kingdom's message to a lamp.

Ancient Middle Eastern lamps were composed of a wick fueled by a vessel filled with oil, similar to Aladdin's Lamp. This candle, or literally "torch," was aflame at night to guide people to shelter. Would anyone light such a candle only to snuff it out under a jar or put it away under a bed? Of course not. The lamp must shine to guide people to safety.

But Jesus enlarges the metaphor of the lamp to burrow into our hearts. Not only does the light shine outside guiding people to the Lord, but it also sheds light inside our hearts—revealing everything. Good thoughts, bad inclinations, and all the uglies show up in that glow. The motivation of the person who keeps the lamp under the bed is also exposed as the Lord says, "Everything hidden will be re-vealed." If we don't appreciate the light of truth, we avoid it, thus losing its benefits.

Jesus graciously warns us in verse 18, "be careful how you listen" to the kingdom message. In other words, Christ is saying, "Listen to my truth, letting it lodge in your hearts. Allow that truth to shine through you, and it will both guide people home to me and reveal your needs." Such is the mercy of God. It cleanses us and lights us like candles for others to find their way.

Revelation 21:23 adds a layer of truth to Christ's teaching concerning the lamp, "The city does not need the sun or the moon to shine on it, for the glory of God gives it light, and *the Lamb is its lamp*." Christ, our sacrificial Lamb is also our Lamp of truth.

When I became a Christian, I thought I would experience constant peace, love, and joy. Instead, the Holy Spirit began a renovation project in my heart, and he's not done yet. Envious thoughts are cowering in corners, dirt lurking beneath the pile of debris, and all manner of evil corrupting my heart. My heart was, and is, a hot mess desperately in need of the searing light of God's truth. Verse 17 says, "For there is nothing hidden that will not be disclosed, and nothing concealed that will not be known or brought out into the open." It sends shivers down my spine. As uncomfortable as letting Jesus shine his light into my heart, it is the only path to freedom from my evil inclinations.

Can you imagine believing in Christ as your Lamp yet smothering that Light by hiding it under a bed? God forbid!

We must carefully read His word, then put it into practice. Jesus wants his light to shine through us. Cast the light of Jesus that all may find their way home to him. Let kingdom truth blaze through you. Whoever shines this light will be given more, and whoever does not will have it taken away. Share Jesus with everyone and let your life overflow with his sparkling light. Keep your lamp lit because the kids aren't all home yet.

Dear Lord, I confess I am a mess. Shine your light inside me and clean me up. I ask that I could be a bright lamp showing your light to those I meet. It is too easy for me to remain quiet when I need to speak up and share your truth. Help me, Lord, I pray in your name. Amen.

"Practice? We're Talkin Bout Practice?"

Now Jesus' mother and brothers came to see him, but they were not able to get near him because of the crowd. Someone told him, "Your mother and brothers are standing outside, wanting to see you."

He replied, "My mother and brothers are those who hear God's word and put it into practice." Luke 8:19-21

"Practice!" basketball legend, Allen Iverson, responded to the reporter's question. "We're talking about practice?"

Infamous for his disdain of practices, Iverson became a great player, immortalized in the Basketball Hall of Fame, through raw talent. But he could never lead his Philadelphia 76ers team to a championship. Listening to coaches and practicing was not a priority, so he never achieved that goal. The Christian life is similar. Implementing God's coaching into our daily routine leads to success.

This passage in Luke stands out as Christ seems to disregard his mother and brothers. But there is a more significant point at play—obedience to God is thicker than blood. The Kingdom of God takes priority over family. This idea contradicts everything drilled into us since we were old enough to breathe. Let's find out why.

No human is more important than Mom. After Christmas and Easter, Mother's Day is the most popular holiday in America. Rightly so, our mothers gave us safe harbors in their wombs from the time we were microscopic cells. Mom birthed us through terrible pain. She sustained us with milk from her body, caressed, taught, disciplined, and healed our wounds until the day adulthood thrust us into the world. It is impossible to overstate a mother's importance to our existence.

But God created us for more than mere survival. We have a destiny and a reason for being. It's what you do with your life that truly honors God, your mother, and your family. Jesus shows how to achieve our eternal purpose. Listen to the Word of God, then do it.

The Nike brand famously coined the phrase, "Just do it." They touched a nerve in America, calling us to get active. Get out and play instead of lounging on the couch. But, our bodies coo to us, "Relax today, chill, sleep in, you deserve it." You can choose to succumb or get active. You know what you should do –just do it.

Jesus has a similar message in spiritual matters. The Greek word "poieo" translates to the phrase, "hear God's word and put it into practice" (verse 21). This verb means to endow a person with a certain quality and bring something to independent existence.

 Practice something over and over until you become it. For instance, practicing piano trains a person to become a pianist. You develop as a professional by performing that occupation. To become a healthy Christian, "practice" doing what the Word of God says. In that transaction, something miraculous happens. You emerge as a faithful Christian.

Was Christ rude to his mother?

No. I think Jesus was saying, "You raised me to be an independent adult and become who God intended me to be. I am doing that now, and that has to come first."

On the journey toward maturity in our faith, we choose to do what God wants rather than what people want. During my senior year at Bible College, I felt an intense internal conflict. I sensed a leading to leave my home in California and start a new church in New England after graduation. But a sinister voice said to me, "How can you minister to people in other places when your mother is not a Christian? That's so hypocritical." I prayed and cried for Mom's salvation, but nothing seemed to happen. This emotional conflict paralyzed me until I recognized the devilish condemnation spoken into my ear. God called me to shed the guilt and seize my God-given calling, trusting him to minister to my mother.

Eventually, I went to the East and pastored several churches during a thirty-five-year career. God drew my mother back to the faith. The Lord loves mothers and gives them the ultimate ministry—to launch their children into their God-ordained purpose. We honor our mother's best by becoming healthy, fruitful, and faithful adults. To do that, we must practice God's Word. Yep, we're talkin' bout practice.

Dear Lord, I want to practice your ways daily. Help me hear your word, chew it, and receive it into my innermost being. Empower me to do what the Bible says even when my flesh doesn't feel like it. Jesus, you were attentive to fulfill your mission, and I ask you for that same focus. I ask this in Christ's name. Amen.

Rising in the Storm

One day Jesus said to his disciples, "Let's go over to the other side of the lake." So they got into a boat and set out. As they sailed, he fell asleep. A squall came down on the lake, so that the boat was being swamped, and they were in great danger.

The disciples went and woke him, saying, "Master, Master, we're going to drown!"

He got up and rebuked the wind and the raging waters; the storm subsided, and all was calm. "Where is your faith?" he asked his disciples.

In fear and amazement they asked one another, "Who is this? He commands even the winds and the water, and they obey him." Luke 8:22–25

When life hits you like a storm, you find out who you are. Recently, I had eyelid surgery. I waited in the hospital hallway in a wheelchair waiting for my wife to pick me up. Woozy, bleeding, and clutching a pain medication prescription, I sat there over an hour feeling like no one in the world cared if I lived or died. Even my cell phone wouldn't work.

Meanwhile, my wife was frantically trying to get to the hospital in a broken-down car. She finally arrived with the bad news. We had to take the car to the shop, then wait all day for repairs before driving two hours through Alabama backwoods back home to Florida. I finally got the pain medication and made it home alive. Anger, frustration, fear, and shame rushed through my mind that day, threatening to overwhelm me.

Luke 8: 23-25 relates a similar story. Christ and the disciples launched out in a boat on the Sea of Galilee when a furious storm threatened to overwhelm them. The disciples rowed hard against the waves and desperately bailed water until they finally decided to wake their sleeping Savior. Three questions emerge from this passage to help us overcome the storms that we face.

The first question boils down to, "Lord, do you care about what I'm going through?"

Look at the disciples as they cry out, "Master, Master, we're sinking. Don't you care that we're going to drown?"

In other words, "Jesus, don't you care about us? We're drowning here. Wake up and pay attention to my needs."

Most of us have experienced painful periods that seemed would never end. The worst is when we feel that nobody cares—not even God. Jesus responds, but not in the way one would expect. What does he do in the storm? Christ talks to it. The Master rebukes the rain, wind, and waves—He acts in the way only God can.

Immediately the world was calm, and the Lord turned to them and asked the second question from our passage, "Where is your faith?"

Their faith was overwhelmed by fear. The problem with fear is it drains us of our confidence in God. Too often, self-preservation kicks in, and our trust in God vanishes at the very time our faith needs to rise and speak to the storm in Christ's name.

Our destiny unfolds according to our faith. To turn to Jesus when our lives, health, finances, or relationships are threatened is essential. Remember, Christ is still at the helm. He still speaks "peace" to storms. Ultimately, our victory does not rest on our faith. It rests squarely on Jesus.

The storm-tossed disciples' story concludes with this third critical question. The disciples asked each other, "Who is this?"

That man sleeping in the boat is the same Jesus who walks on water. He speaks to the deaf, and they hear. He makes mud from spit and heals the blind. This Savior commands the stormy sea to calm down, the paralyzed man to rise, and the guilty women to "go and sin no more." He speaks honestly to the crooked, peacefully to the angry, and comforts the lonely. This man in the boat is the Son of God.

Together these three questions ask us, "How is your soul?" Internal turmoil mars the landscape of our hearts. Bitterness fouls our waters. Regret and doubt blur our vision, but Jesus speaks the word of peace and brings calm to our storm-tossed souls. Christ commands even the tempests to be still, and peace settles. Breathe in the fresh wind of the Spirit and hear the word of the Peacemaker that calms the situation. Jesus is the man in your boat.

My Lord, open my eyes that I may see who you are. Sometimes, I feel so overwhelmed; I forget that you are in the boat with me. I may not have the faith I should, but I know I have you. I trust you to bring me through, one storm at a time, one day at a time, one situation at a time. Jesus, I know you care. My faith may be absent at times, but I know who you are, my Peacemaker.

Freedom, Fear,
and Faith

*They sailed to the region of the Gerasenes,
which is across the lake from Galilee. When Jesus
stepped ashore, he was met by a demon-possessed
man from the town. For a long time this man had
not worn clothes or lived in a house, but had lived
in the tombs. When he saw Jesus, he cried out and
fell at his feet, shouting at the top of his voice,
"What do you want with me, Jesus, Son of the
Most High God? I beg you, don't torture me!" For
Jesus had commanded the evil spirit to come out
of the man. Many times it had seized him, and
though he was chained hand and foot and kept under guard, he had broken his chains and had been
driven by the demon into solitary places.*

Jesus asked him, "What is your name?"

"Legion," he replied, because many demons had gone into him. And they begged him repeatedly not to order them to go into the Abyss.

A large herd of pigs was feeding there on the hillside. The demons begged Jesus to let them go into them, and he gave them permission. When the demons came out of the man, they went into the pigs, and the herd rushed down the steep bank into the lake and was drowned.

When those tending the pigs saw what had happened, they ran off and reported this in the town and countryside, and the people went out to see what had happened. When they came to Jesus, they found the man from whom the demons had gone out, sitting at Jesus' feet, dressed and in his right mind; and they were afraid. Those who had seen it told the people how the demon-possessed man had been cured. Then all the people of the region of the Gerasenes asked Jesus to leave them, because they were overcome with fear. So he got into the boat and left.

The man from whom the demons had gone out begged to go with him, but Jesus sent him away, saying, "Return home and tell how much God has done for you." So the man went away and told all over town how much Jesus had done for him. Luke 8:26-39

The disciples shook with awe wondering what manner of man could speak peace to a raging storm.

When they stepped off the boat, the craziest person they ever saw rushed Jesus shouting, "What do you want with me Jesus, Son of the Most-High God?" Storm by sea. Storm by man. Storm by devils. The worst of all? The human storm brewing.

Christ led his disciples across the Sea of Galilee for one seriously messed up man. He loves us, even those consumed with evil.

Plagued with seizures, mental illness, and evil spirits, the demon-possessed man self-identified as "Legion." A Roman legion consisted of 6,800 fighting men, so we know a large mob of demons resided in this man. He seems most hopeless until Jesus arrived and spoke to the devils.

The demons begged Christ not to send them into the "Abyss," the ancient prison for those fallen angels who rebelled against God. They asked Jesus instead to send them into a herd of pigs, the animal the Jews were forbidden to eat. Jesus sent the demons into the swine, and they hurled themselves down the hillside into the sea where they drowned. Evil always ends in destruction.

We can be sure the swine herders weren't happy with their financial loss. Yet, here sat the crazy naked guy clothed and in his right mind at Christ's feet listening to the Rabbi's words. Eyewitnesses were spreading the news of the miracle in the village of the Gerasenes. The people responded with fear rather than faith. While fear demands that Christ leave, the freedman begs to stay with him. True faith clings to Jesus.

"Return home and tell how much God has done for you," Christ commands in verse 39. Out with the insanity and into the ministry. Jesus sends the man home to the village that had only known him as a madman. Imagine the story he had to tell.

The most potent witness a person can give is their testimony. Luke chronicles in the Book of Acts the ministry of Paul as the great apostle preaches through the Middle East and Europe. Five times Paul recounts his testimony of salvation. Along with the insane man and Paul, our witness is a powerful tool in God's hands.

We are all on a journey from bondage to faith in Jesus. Unfortunately, our path usually proceeds through places that evoke terror. Those who face their fear come out the other side with a testimony that will move others to believe in Jesus. Just ask the disciples who have now met the tempest at sea and the storm of the devil. Their day is not over as they are about to face the whirlwind of the crowds.

The people in Gerasene rejected Christ despite the miracle they had just seen. They demanded Christ leave. Why? "All the people of the region of the Gerasenes asked Jesus to leave them because they were overcome with fear" (verse 37.) Fear robbed them of the greatest blessing in the history of humanity. Another motive lurks beneath the veneer of their rejection of Christ—the demise of their large herd of pigs and the subsequent financial loss. The old saying applies, "When it comes to love, or money, love is bound to lose." Such is the way of the world.

The Lord shows us a better way as Revelation 12:11 says, "They overcame him [the devil] by the blood of the Lamb and by the word of their testimony." Jesus has given us freedom from the devil and fear. Our confidence against the devil and the world rests in our witness to Christ's work in our lives.

Deliver me of my craziness Lord, I know I need you. I cling to you, my Savior, help me to face my bondage and my fears. I give them to you and ask for the courage to believe in you. Deliver me from the love of money so that I never miss what you are doing in my life. I want to be a bold witness where I am. In your name, I pray. Amen.

A Tale of Two Daughters

Now when Jesus returned, a crowd welcomed him, for they were all expecting him. Then a man named Jairus, a ruler of the synagogue, came and fell at Jesus' feet, pleading with him to come to his house because his only daughter, a girl of about twelve, was dying.

As Jesus was on his way, the crowds almost crushed him. And a woman was there who had been subject to bleeding for twelve years, but no one could heal her. She came up behind him and touched the edge of his cloak, and immediately her bleeding stopped.

"Who touched me?" Jesus asked.

When they all denied it, Peter said, "Master, the people are crowding and pressing against you."

But Jesus said, "Someone touched me; I know that power has gone out from me."

Then the woman, seeing that she could not go unnoticed, came trembling and fell at his feet. In the presence of all the people, she told why she had touched him and how she had been instantly healed. Then he said to her, "Daughter, your faith has healed you. Go in peace."

While Jesus was still speaking, someone came from the house of Jairus, the synagogue ruler. "Your daughter is dead," he said. "Don't bother the teacher anymore."

Hearing this, Jesus said to Jairus, "Don't be afraid; just believe, and she will be healed."

When he arrived at the house of Jairus, he did not let anyone go in with him except Peter, John and James, and the child's father and mother. Meanwhile, all the people were wailing and mourning for her. "Stop wailing," Jesus said. "She is not dead but asleep."

They laughed at him, knowing that she was dead. But he took her by the hand and said, "My child, get up!" Her spirit returned, and at once she stood up. Then Jesus told them to give her something to eat. Her parents were astonished, but he ordered them not to tell anyone what had happened. Luke 8:40-55

Desperate people get God's attention. Luke recounts the story of two daughters, and it is in the connection of the two healings that draw us into the tidal wave of Christ's compassion. The characters here show us how to respond to the demanding situations many of us face. Igniting faith in God's great love for His children is the purpose of the gospel, especially for those in distressed circumstances.

Jairus was a man of significant influence in his community. As the "ruler of the synagogue" (verse 41), his peers typically showed him respect and admiration. Nevertheless, this desperate dad throws himself on the ground before Jesus. For twelve years, his home rang with the joy and laughter only a child can bring, and now his little girl lies dying. Sometimes, life makes us cry.

Jairus' urgent attempt to bring the Healer to his home is interrupted. "Who touched me?" Christ asks as he comes to a sudden stop.

I can almost hear Jairus silently screaming inside his head. *Don't stop Jesus! My baby is fading, come on, my daughter n-e-e-d-s you.* Another person arrested Christ's attention, one quite different from Jairus and his daughter—a ceremonially unclean woman, continually hemorrhaging blood, enters the gospel story. The Scriptures banned her from worship. It forbade her to contact anyone, even her husband and children. For twelve years, she lived as an outcast. The woman exhausted her money in search of a medical solution. Sometimes, life makes us bleed.

Miserable, lonely, and despairing, the drained woman illegally pressed through the crowd and touched Jesus bringing everyone to a breathless halt. Desperate people do desperate things.

Jairus must have been infuriated. This woman started bleeding the same year his daughter was born. The visit takes place about the time his daughter would begin her female monthly cycle. Their similarities were uncanny. Their separate threads were knit together by their pressing needs and their hope in Jesus.

"Then He [Christ] said to her, "Daughter, your faith has healed you. Go in peace" (verse 48.) While Jairus worried about his daughter, Jesus calls this believing woman with the familial name, "Daughter." Her actions demonstrated her faith. She reached out and touched the fringe of Christ's robe, and her faith gave her entrance to God's family.

The original Greek word translated "touched" literally means "attached." Her faith moved her to grab or clutch Christ. Note to Jairus—lay hold of Jesus by faith!

Meanwhile, Jairus' daughter died. As the women wailed and the mourners moaned, Jesus encouraged Jairus, "Don't be afraid; just believe, and she will be healed" (verse 50.) Christ expects living, vital faith from us. Jesus calls to the dead girl, "Get up, my child!" Life floods into her being, and her spirit revives.

Father God looked upon this dad's faith. Resurrection erupted. Mercy also flowed to the unclean woman whom Jesus calls "Daughter." Christ touched the dying girl. The woman touched Jesus. Jarius' daughter lived twelve years, died, and then resurrected. The cast-out woman was dying for twelve years and then fully lived. God is the Father of all who believe. He draws near to those who desperately reach out to Him. Sometimes, life amazes us.

Dear Lord, give me a heart to desperately seek You. I know that my heart is cold, and my eyes are dry. Ignite me today with fiery faith that I would not be lukewarm. I ask that you heal the hurts and memories that have left me bleeding and drained. I put my trust in you today, believing that you are making my life a miracle. I stand in awe of what you have done in these daughters, and I anticipate more extraordinary things yet to come. Thank you, Lord. Amen.

Power and Authority

When Jesus had called the Twelve together, he gave them power and authority to drive out all demons and to cure diseases, and he sent them out to preach the kingdom of God and to heal the sick. He told them: "Take nothing for the journey — no staff, no bag, no bread, no money, no extra tunic. Whatever house you enter, stay there until you leave that town. If people do not welcome you, shake the dust off your feet when you leave their town, as a testimony against them." So they set out and went from village to village, preaching the gospel and healing people everywhere. Luke 9:1-6

Evangelist Milton Elithorpe was an elderly minister on staff at Angelus Temple, the Los Angles church I attended as a young Christian. An electrifying preacher would often invite people to pray at the altar to respond to his message. As they knelt, Brother Elithorpe would pass by and gently lay his hand on their shoulders, praying that God would heal them of any sickness and forgive their sins. He personified enthusiasm, integrity, and compassion.

I later learned the source of Brother Elithorpe's passion. As a college student in the 1930s living in downtown Los Angeles, he got hit by a car while walking to school. The impact threw him seventeen feet through the air. An ambulance rushed him to the hospital, where they found his interior organs crushed, leaving little hope. Medical personnel was not able to stem the flow of internal bleeding. So, they put him in an ambulance and took him, still vomiting blood, to a church known for praying for the sick.

The young Elithorpe was wheeled into that great church on a gurney during a worship service. The service stopped, and everyone gathered around him. They laid hands on him and prayed. The power of God completely healed him.

Fifty years later, I would have been skeptical had I not met the man and others in attendance when God touched him. Decades later, he still preached with the gusto of a teenager because God transformed his life. The Almighty rescued him from a painful death and delivered him from sin. The healing power of Jesus burned in his soul and ministry for the remainder of his life.

Jesus cares enough to convey the ministry of healing to his disciples. This passage in Luke shows Christ challenging the Disciples to take the next step of leadership. He sends them out to test their faith. Could the power and authority of the Lord work through them as through Jesus? Undeniably, it did. They witnessed Christ deliver people plagued by demons. They saw Jesus heal the unhealable and raise the dead, and consequently, Jesus sent them out to the surrounding villages. He gives them a few simple instructions.

The instructions Jesus gave are worth noting, "Take nothing for the journey." He sent them with no money, and no backup plan, only their faith in God. In effect, he said to them, trust the God who knows the number of hairs on your head to meet your needs. When you can trust God to meet your needs, it's not so hard to believe that he will meet the needs of others. That is the place where ministry is born.

The second instruction given the disciples was to live in a place of peace. If you don't have peace with those you visit, either fix-it or move on. Don't look back. Don't waste time on people who are disagreeable with the message you carry. You cannot control how people respond to you. I think Christ is saying the peace of God you have is most precious. Carefully guard your peace even as you give it away to people who will receive it. The world knows trouble and turmoil, but you need to live in a place of peace.

Preaching and healing are the activities of kingdom-minded people. The word "preaching" in Luke

9:6 comes from two root words. The beginning of the term originates from the Hebrew "eua," where we get the name "Eve," meaning "life-giver." The middle of the word, "aggelos," conveys the idea of declaring the good news. Together these words mean sharing a life-giving message with words. The challenge for Christians is engaging in this kingdom work.

Christ commissions his followers to a second companion work—healing. The word "healing" from Luke 9:6 translates the Greek word "therapon," from which we get the English word "therapy." This verb means to "wait upon menially with heat." Think of a nurse who administers a hot pad to an aching muscle, and you have the idea. Christians apply the healing therapy of Jesus to hurting people. With the anointing of the Holy Spirit, we can humbly invoke the healing fire of God to sickness, disease, and heartache.

The Catholic Evangelist, Saint Francis of Assisi said, "Preach the gospel at all times and if necessary, use words." The idea being when witnessing to others, we don't necessarily have to speak out the message of the gospel. But Luke 9:6 demonstrates that sharing the good news is a verbal activity. Sharing the gospel with your words accompanied by healing prayer are the building blocks of the kingdom. Demonstrate God's power and authority by voicing his Word.

Brother Elithorpe's life was transformed when he encountered the healing power of God. He gave God's grace, peace, and healing to people with an unwavering zeal for the rest of his life. This mantle of ministry imparted to the Disciples has passed through the ages to us. We cannot drop the baton of Christ's power and authority. Pass it on, friends.

Oh Lord, make me an agent of the kingdom of God. Use my prayers to heal the sick and my words to proclaim the life-giving news of Jesus the Savior. May you fuel my passion with peace, integrity, grace, and love. In your name, I pray. Amen.

The Most Important Question

Now Herod the tetrarch heard about all that was going on. And he was perplexed, because some were saying that John had been raised from the dead, others that Elijah had appeared, and still others that one of the prophets of long ago had come back to life. But Herod said, "I beheaded John. Who, then, is this I hear such things about?" And he tried to see him.

-When the apostles returned, they reported to Jesus what they had done. Then he took them with him and they withdrew by themselves to a town called Bethsaida, but the crowds learned about it and followed him. He welcomed them and

> *spoke to them about the kingdom of God, and*
> *healed those who needed healing. Luke 9:1-11*

Not everyone who claims to be a Christian is sincere. Many talk the talk but don't walk the walk. Herod Antipas, in our passage, fits in that category. He had a genuine interest in Christ but would not allow transformative faith to change his life.

Luke presented Christ in Chapter 8 as Master of the storms; Deliverer of the demon-afflicted; Healer of the hemorrhage-plagued woman, and Raiser of the dead. No wonder Herod asks, "Who is this man?"

Jesus is at the pinnacle of his public ministry, touching the multitudes with miraculous grace and power.

In contrast to Christ's gracious gifts of mercy, Herod, the tetrarch (governor), stands as a diabolical figure. He was a frivolous and vain ruler and was chargeable with evil (Mark 8:15; Luke 3:19; Luke 13:31 Luke 13:32). He divorced his wife to marry his brother's wife, Herodias. When John the Baptist calls him out on his adultery, Herod arrests him. Later, Herod succumbs to the wiles of his stepdaughter's party dance. Excited by her performance, he grants her wish for John's head on a platter, which she gives to her mother, Herodias.

Luke documents an interaction between Herod and Christ later in Luke 23:6-12, where he shows an interest in Christ's ministry. Obviously "perplexed" by his guilt for killing John the Baptist, he lacks the inner fortitude to set Jesus free. Herod, slave of his passions, does not have the integrity to act according to the truth standing before him.

Herod reflects the inner turmoil many of us feel. We want to know this miraculous Christ, but we struggle with hidden passions. Many struggles originate from sexual desires, others from greed, and some from pride. If people dare to criticize us, pride jumps to defend us so fast we miss the criticism's nugget of truth. Arrogance blinds us to our faults.

Herod was a man plagued by a well-earned guilty conscience. He imagined Christ was John the Baptist raised from the dead come back to haunt him. Shakespeare said through Hamlet, "Conscience doth make cowards of us all." A guilt-ridden conscience makes dead men's voice ring in our heads, and the opinions of others feel like attacks.

When people are critical of me, I often react badly. Flushed with anger, defensive, and wounded, I justify my position. These feelings leave me emotionally drained and spiritually frozen. The Lord has shown me that my reactions are born of pride and built walls of self-protection that shielded me from the changes God wanted to make in me. I eventually turned toward God, leaving me vulnerable to his searching presence. In the presence of the Lord I experience love, acceptance, and forgiveness. These empower me to change.

Luke contrasts the returning Disciples to the evil Herod. They return from their ministry assignment. Jesus withdraws with them to a place of retreat, Bethsaida. But the crowds learn of the Lord's location and interrupt their respite. Jesus does what

Jesus does–he accepts them and serves them. Christ welcomes the people, teaches, and heals them with no thought to his needs. Not only that, as we'll see in tomorrow's devotion, he also feeds them.

> *My God, Herod is evil. Unfortunately, I feel like I am related to him. Lord. Please destroy the foundations of guilt and defensiveness in me– these prevent me from surrendering to your grace. Your mercy overwhelms my sin, and your love is more tangible. Thank you, Lord, that you are who you are. Amen.*

More Than Enough

Late in the afternoon the Twelve came to him and said, "Send the crowd away so they can go to the surrounding villages and countryside and find food and lodging, because we are in a remote place here."

He replied, "You give them something to eat."

They answered, "We have only five loaves of bread and two fish — unless we go and buy food for all this crowd." (About five thousand men were there.)

But he said to his disciples, "Have them sit down in groups of about fifty each." The disciples did so, and everybody sat down. Taking the five loaves and the two fish and looking up to heaven, he gave thanks and broke them. Then he gave them to the disciples to set before the people. They all ate and were satisfied, and the disciples picked up twelve basketfuls of broken pieces that were left over. Luke 9:12-17

Our lives consist of a constant search for more. More food. More stuff. More excitement. A reporter asked the late, wealthy industrialist John D. Rockefeller how much money it takes to be happy. He snapped back, "Just a little bit more."

God is more than enough. The ancient Hebrew Scriptures describe God as "El Shaddai" (Genesis 17:1), meaning "the all-sufficient God who is more than enough."

Christ commissions His disciples in Luke 9:1-17 and sends them on a preaching journey with no luggage, no food, and no money. It is a lesson in trusting God's provision. They demonstrated their faith in God when they prayed for the sick and shared the good news. Their success was so pronounced it reached the ears of Herod, the tetrarch. Christ's message multiplied exponentially as His twelve disciples obeyed. The crowds following Jesus swelled to over fifteen thousand people. Everything was swell until they all got hungry.

"Send the crowd away so they can go to the surrounding villages and countryside and find food and lodging," the disciples whined to Jesus in Luke 9:12. The same Disciples who had seen Jesus heal the multitudes saw this present need as too

overwhelming. Jesus is in the faith-expanding business. They were in Faith class 101,

"Jesus replied to them, 'You give them something to eat.'"

They answered, "We have only five loaves of
bread and two fish – unless we go and buy food for
all this crowd."

Jesus understood the vast reservoir of God's provision while the disciples only saw their limited resources. Christ had compassion upon the people,
while the disciples saw them as a burden.

Several years ago, while I pastored in Massachusetts, our church sponsored a "Park Party" in an im-
poverished neighborhood. We provided free
haircuts, bike repair, activities, games, and prizes
for children and young people. At the conclusion,
we planned to share the gospel and feed the folks
hot dogs, chips, and soda. We prepared for six hundred people, but the crowd grew to over a thousand
hungry souls. Internally, my heart raced, and I
shouted silently, "Lord, what are we going to do?"

I paced the park, wringing my hands until we finished feeding the people. "Hey, Pastor, everyone
got a hotdog. We never ran out." Somehow, God
turned our six hundred wieners and buns into a
thousand. That's God-math. El Shaddai is more than
enough, and Jesus never fails.

Too many Christians believe in a chastising God
with an abundance of lightning bolts flashing at the
slightest provocation. That is the Greek god Zeus,
not the Christian God. The Lord gave us His Son to
save us rather than rain fire and brimstone in judgment. His mercy is unfathomable, and his grace

generous. The Lord is all-sufficient, content, fulfilled. God is more than enough for you and the needs of your friends and family.

Meanwhile, back in Galilee, Jesus broke the five loaves of bread and the two fish handing the pieces to the Disciples for distribution. The thousands present all ate. The greatest miracle of all—they were satisfied. They all partook with twelve full baskets of food leftover, one for each disciple. They continued to eat from the overflow of God's blessing. The Lord has bread for you, too–more than enough to share.

O Lord, my faith is too small. Please give me a vision for those who have needs that you want me to address. It is easy for me to say, "send them away," while you want to reveal your extraordinary power and provision. I am in awe of you, "El Shaddai." Do it again, Lord, in our time and place. I offer my hands to help distribute the bread and carry the baskets. In your name, I pray. Amen.

The Power of Blessing

Then He took the five loaves and the two fish, and looking up to heaven, He blessed and broke them, and gave them to the disciples to set before the multitude. So they all ate... Luke 9:16-17

A basketball in my hands is worth about fifteen dollars, but it's worth over eighty million bucks in Lebron James' hands. I can buy a decent football for a hundred dollars and toss it around the yard, but that same ball in Tom Brady's hands is solid gold. Five loaves and two fish in my hands are a decent lunch, but in Christ's hand, it feeds the multitudes with baskets leftover. But how does he do it?

Jesus *takes* the five loaves and two fish, *breaks* them, and *speaks a blessing* to God. What Christ takes, he returns multiplied. Eons ago, he took the Earth's dust and formed humanity into a living, breathing soul. The Master also spat on the ground and took the mud to heal a blind man's eyes. Jesus uses natural objects to make something new and beautiful. So, why are we so reluctant to allow him to take our lives, break us, and multiply us?

Thousands of eager followers hung on Christ's every word all day in a remote place. Now they were hungry. The Disciples have barely enough food for themselves. The Lord took the Disciple's food in his hands and broke it. He looked toward heaven and lifted the loaves to God with a blessing. This occasion is when they would learn the thanksgiving blessing makes all the difference.

The Greek word translated "blessing" in this passage is *eulogeo,* meaning to speak well. It is the same word used in the Greek translation of the Old Testament when God looked upon creation and said, "It is good."

Jesus surrendered the meager resource in his hands—loaves of bread—and spoke well of it. He called what God had provided "good," even in the face of thousands of hungry people. Therein lies the miracle.

If you surrender your life to God and speak well of it, you will be a candidate for his blessing.

I remember a high school-aged young man named Rodney at a Christian youth camp in New Hampshire. I served as the camp director many years ago. Rodney came from a troubled home in a rough section of Boston. He always seemed to find trouble and generally was a nuisance.

One evening, after the revival meeting, Rodney was stirring up trouble in the back of the chapel. Prompted by the Lord, I approached him and put my hand on his shoulder. I looked into his eyes and spoke a blessing by telling him all the good qualities I saw in him. I thanked God for sending him to youth camp. I expounded on the great things God wanted to do in his life. Then, I walked away, leaving him in God's hands.

Back to Jesus and the hungry people, watch what happens next as Christ *broke* the loaves and the fish. It's in the breaking that multiplication occurs. Jesus does the same thing with people–he breaks them to make them grow.

If it sounds like the Christian life is a breaking process, your hearing is excellent. As Jesus broke the loaves and the fish, they multiplied in his hands, and he gave them away. The Lord breaks us so he can dedicate us to the service of love.

Blessing flows to us from God when we allow him to break us—just ask Jesus. He was wounded for our transgressions, shattered in the garden of Gethsemane, and crushed on the cross. Christ is the ultimate demonstration of brokenness that produces miraculous fruitfulness.

Sometimes, fruitfulness can only come through brokenness. Author and pastor J.R. Miller said, "Christ is building His kingdom with earth's broken things. Men want only the strong, the successful, and the victorious in building their kingdoms. But God is the God of the unsuccessful and of the failures. Heaven is filling with earth's broken lives, and there is no bruised reed that Christ cannot take and restore to glorious blessedness and beauty. He can take the life crushed by pain or sorrow and make it into a harp whose music shall be all praise. He can lift earth's saddest failure up to heaven's glory."

Christ wanted to feed the multitudes, so he took the small portions in his hands, broke them, and gave the fragments away. Not only were the people fed, but there were also twelve baskets of food leftover. Without the activities blessing and breaking, there would have been no miracle.

Taking, breaking, and blessing is God's formula for success. Allow Jesus to take your life. Surrender to him. Christ will receive you and break you–he will wash out every remnant of sin from you. Then he will speak a blessing–offering you up to God like the loaves and fish. That's when extraordinary begins to happen.

Remember Rodney? Our paths crossed again some twenty years later. My daughter and grandson went to a youth camp in Southern Ohio. They were excited to be there because an exciting young preacher was scheduled to preach. The preacher's name? Rodney. Yep, the same trouble-maker Rodney I knew long ago. He told my daughter the blessing that I spoke into his life changed him and turned him toward the Lord. Never underestimate the power your words of thanksgiving have toward God and others.

My Jesus, I surrender my life to you. Please speak a blessing over me like you did the loaves and the fish. Take me, break me, and give me to those who need your grace. Sometimes it's difficult to see your hands working through it all. In your name, I pray. Amen.

The Great Revelation

Once when Jesus was praying in private and his disciples were with him, he asked them, "Who do the crowds say I am?"

They replied, "Some say John the Baptist; others say Elijah; and still others, that one of the prophets of long ago has come back to life."

"But what about you?" he asked. "Who do you say I am?"

Peter answered, "The Christ of God."

Jesus strictly warned them not to tell this to anyone. And he said, "The Son of Man must suffer many things and be rejected by the elders, chief priests and teachers of the law, and he must

be killed and on the third day be raised to life."
Luke 9:18-22

Eventually, everyone must come to the revelation of Christ. Before I became a Christian, some new-found friends from a church youth group invited me to a concert. I was disappointed that none of them showed up to hear Andre Crouch and the Disciples, then the hottest contemporary Christian group around. Still, I stayed and listened to the music.

I sat alone in the packed auditorium. About five hundred people crowded into the old hall built for twelve hundred people. They swayed to the music with their hands lifted. Spontaneous "Hallelujahs" rang out. The floor vibrated, and the room shimmered with emotion.

Beyond the music was a powerful dynamic that moved me. As I was not yet a Christian, all this seemed so foreign. Halfway through the concert, my heart raced, frantic with what felt like fear. Overwhelmed by my feelings and uneased by the demonstration of emotion around me, I quickly ran to the door. I couldn't take the spiritual heat.

Scampering the five miles home on my Honda scooter, my mind cried out, *why are you running? What scared you so much you had to run out?* I realized then I was running from God.

Sixteen years old, wearing my high school letterman's jacket to bolster my machismo, and an agnostic, I was trying to escape the Lord. By the time

I arrived home, I had come up with excuses for why I would not become a Christian.

I mentally protested, *what about all the hypocrites in the church?* I didn't know Christian hypocrites but had heard about them on TV. I opened our dusty family Bible to a random place, stuck my finger down on the first verse I saw, "Look not at the other people in the church."

Wow! That's God speaking to me through the Bible. God is real. My time of revelation had come.

I decided to go forward that next Sunday in church and give my life to the Lord.

In the passage above, Jesus asks, "Who do the crowds say that I am?" The casual observations of the crowds concerning Jesus were favorable. The prophet heals people, delivers the oppressed, and feeds the masses. What more could they ask? They had a partial understanding of Jesus but not one that would sustain them through the trials ahead.

The great question Doctor Luke sets before us next is, "Who do you say I am?" As Christ wraps up his ministry in Galilee, his disciples must come to understand who he is before he ascends to Jerusalem and the cross. The disciples must follow Jesus into the crucifixion's fiery trial, and they will need a revelation of Christ's true nature and mission.

Jesus queries the disciples deeply. Beyond the Law of Moses, past their experience of Christ's miracles, the Lord presses his finger into their core belief. "Who do you say that I am?"

"Peter answered, 'The Christ of God.'" His response thunders through history. The great revelation to Peter by the Spirit reflects his discovery.

Christianity is not about understanding a creed, doctrine, or lifestyle. It is about knowing the identity of Jesus Christ as the Messiah, Anointed of God, Waymaker, and Miracle-worker. Once you know him, there is no turning back. Then the hammer falls.

Jesus is rejected, suffers, killed, and raised back to life. The more profound revelation of Jesus is The Way of the Cross that Christ must travel. The disclosure of Jesus concerns the destiny of the Suffering Messiah. Over and over, Jesus tells the Disciples he has a purpose to fulfill. Luke explicitly records Christ's descriptions of his suffering, death, and resurrection three times, Luke 9:22, Luke 7:25, and Luke 24:7.

Luke's gospel shows Christ making this prophetic declaration early in his ministry. Dietrich Bonhoeffer said, "The cross is not the terrible end to an otherwise god-fearing and happy life, but it meets us at the beginning of our communion with Christ."

Why were the disciples so surprised when they learned that Jesus must suffer? Because he was telling them things they didn't want to hear.

How often does God speak to us, but we don't hear him because we don't want to listen? Often.

Does the Lord warn us of things we should avoid, but we do what we want to do? Yes.

Does the Spirit's guidance blow past us because we don't stop to acknowledge Jesus is our Lord when it comes to our decisions? Yes, regularly.

Accepting Jesus Christ is the beginning of the great revelation. That acceptance also means following him wherever he leads. The Lord wants to take us deeper into The Way of the Cross, as the next chapter shows. Stay tuned.

> *O Lord my God, I want to hear your voice. I long to have the Spirit reveal more of who you are. Please give me ears to know your voice and eyes to see your revelation. I confess today that I am willing to follow you on the way of the cross. Amen.*

The Cross Shapes You

Then he said to them all: "If anyone would come after me, he must deny himself and take up his cross daily and follow me. For whoever wants to save his life will lose it, but whoever loses his life for me will save it. What good is it for a man to gain the whole world, and yet lose or forfeit his very self? If anyone is ashamed of me and my words, the Son of Man will be ashamed of him when he comes in his glory and in the glory of the Father and of the holy angels. I tell you the truth, some who are standing here will not taste death before they see the kingdom of God."

Luke 9:23-27

An old story describes a young Christian who experiences a traumatic trial. He begs the Lord in prayer to remove his terrible cross. Heaven seems hardened to his plight, so he goes to bed with a burdened heart. The man tosses and turns in a night of fitful sleep. Dreams of faraway lands float in his mind. He sees himself strolling beside Christ on a lush, green mountain road, and the young man pours out all his difficulties. They journey over the summit where a panorama of a vast valley of white crosses lay before them.

Jesus breaks the silence, "Everyone who follows Me will have a cross to bear even as all who enter My kingdom will suffer trials."

"My cross is so difficult," the young man said. "It's not fair. Let me have another cross to bear."

"Pick the one you want," Christ said, then waved his arm towards the endless sea of crosses small and great.

They walked silently among the crosses for a long time until the man lighted upon a tiny cross.

"I'll take this one," He decided.

Christ stepped forward and pulled the little cross up from its base. The Lord scrutinized it, and there, at the bottom, a name was written. Jesus smiled, looked up, and said, "Why this is your name. This is the cross you have been bearing all along."

With that, the dream ended.

A cross-less Christianity is the hidden temptation of our faith. By nature, Christianity entails the idea of sacrificial living for the higher good of others. Many people look at Christianity as the means to a happier life, a tranquil family, more money, and better health. But a crucified Savior is not well served by self-indulging people.

What are our crosses?

They are not just trials, or hardships, or even sickness. A cross is sometimes the persecution that comes from following in Christ's steps. At times, it is bearing the disdain that accompanies those who walk in the narrow way of Jesus. When we choose to sacrifice our time, emotions, and money for others, we serve our Savior well. Confessing Christ means we embrace His death, and we accept the reality of a cross for ourselves.

Christianity is an abiding faith that produces a dependent belief in Jesus. A talking relationship with Christ inevitably leads to a cross. Not a pretty silver piece of jewelry you hang on your neck or the wall, but a death-inducing cross.

The Christ-like life begins when we put to death our self-will and yield to Christ as King. When we banish self-centeredness and give our lives to serve others, we submit to Christ as Lord.

God gave us free will so we could freely love. When you choose to offer up your right of choice, you are surrendering your life and making room for love. Whenever I'm losing in my life, I'm learning to fight the impulse to strive. Instead, I am beginning to ask, "Lord, where do I need to surrender fully? What do I need to sacrifice for your love to win in this situation?

The cross of Christ is not only an instrument of death to self, but it is the entrance into His resurrection life. You will experience the vitality of Christ's present life as you identify with His death and all it accomplished.

Paul wrote in Romans 6:11-13 (NIV), "Count yourselves dead to sin but alive to God in Christ Jesus...offer yourselves to God, as those who have been brought from death to life." Many say that Christianity is a religion of losers. Yes, it is. Christians are people who chose to lose their life to gain an eternal dimension to life. The cross shapes you into the image of Christ—a sacrificial demonstration of the love of God.

We have victory in this life and that which is to come through Christ's work on the cross. Through the cross, forgiveness, salvation, healing, and hope flow freely. It gives us ultimate triumph over our final enemy—death. We have peace with God and acceptance into His holy family. Our recovery, redemption, and reconciliation were paid for by Christ's sacrifice. Hallelujah! The cross is not just a past accomplishment. It is the present activity of God in our lives, molding us into Christians who live like Christ.

My God, it doesn't feel good to be chiseled into the likeness of Christ, but oh, how I long for it. I accept the crosses you have for me to bear. Let my trials form me so that I will live in the sacrificial manner of your son. In his name, I pray. Amen.

The Light and the Glory

About eight days after Jesus said this, he took Peter, John and James with him and went up onto a mountain to pray. As he was praying, the appearance of his face changed, and his clothes became as bright as a flash of lightning. Two men, Moses and Elijah, appeared in glorious splendor, talking with Jesus. They spoke about his departure, which he was about to bring to fulfillment at Jerusalem. Peter and his companions were very sleepy, but when they became fully awake, they saw his glory and the two men standing with him. As the men were leaving Jesus, Peter said to him, "Master, it is good for us to be here. Let us put up three shelters-one for you, one for Moses and one for Elijah." (He did not know what he was saying.)

While he was speaking, a cloud appeared and enveloped them, and they were afraid as they entered the cloud. A voice came from the cloud, saying, "This is my Son, whom I have chosen; listen to him." When the voice had spoken, they found that Jesus was alone. The disciples kept this to themselves, and told no one at that time what they had seen. Luke 9:28-36

The Light of Life suddenly shines through as Luke depicts the dynamic reality of Christ's inner presence—Light of very Light—housed in a fleshy tent. In the essence of his being, Jesus the Son of God *is* light (John 1). That reality comes shining through on the Mount of Transfiguration. Luke's Gospel positions the Transfiguration of Jesus as the culmination of Peter's declaration of Christ as the Son of God and the preparation for His passion. For us, it is the debut of our destiny.

The disciples were sleepily unaware as the miracle unfolds. They awakened to witness the glory of God displayed, lustrous light and voluminous voice unveiled! We drowsily meander through our lives oblivious to God working beyond the curtain of our consciousness. *Lord, help us see your splendor in our day.*

The spiritual life of Christ laid bare before us in this passage is extraordinary. Add to that, Moses and Elijah unveiled in their brilliance. The resurrected prophets are recognizable yet demonstrate that eternal life looks radiant. Jesus came not only to reveal His glory but to impart that timeless dimension of life to us so that the same splendor can reside in us. Paul explains, "And we, who with unveiled faces all reflect the Lord's glory, are being transformed into his likeness with ever-increasing glory." (2 Corinthians 3:13-18a)

Heaven is your destiny, and its glory is growing inside you now. God wants to demonstrate His presence in you to others. 2 Corinthians 4:11 says, "For we who are alive are always being given over to death for Jesus' sake, so that his life may be revealed in our mortal body." The struggles you are experiencing have a divine purpose and plan—to make known God's glory in you.

The cloud enveloping the disciples is striking. The Voice of the Holy Spirit spoke from the mist divulging the identity of Jesus to the disciples and us. This scene illustrates the whole purpose of the gospel, God showing us His Son and gathering us into His presence.

Years ago, while in a vulnerable place in my life, I had a dream. I saw myself as a little boy, about six years old. I was running happy and free, with the wind blowing through my hair. I felt like I had just had my hair cut—slick and clean. I was satisfied, too, with bubble gum in my mouth like old-time barbers would give kids who behaved well. In the dream, I raced toward a white, puffy cloud. As I ran up to it, I leaped into the mist. Enveloped by that billowy mass, I intuitively knew that it was God. Utterly enclosed in His presence, I felt Him say, "I love you, my son."

The revelations of God bear out his love for his children. The Father sent Moses and Elijah to prepare Jesus for his redemptive mission. He also revealed Christ's glory to lavish that same type of love upon those who have put their faith in Jesus.

Father God, I hear your voice telling me to listen to your dear son, Jesus. It is so hard for me to be quiet and heed the words of your Son. Please help me, Lord. May I see the light and the glory of Christ, and may I hear your voice affirming me as your child. It is difficult for me to imagine that you would say you love me as your son after knowing all I have done. I put my faith in the glory of Jesus today as I stand in his light. In your name, I pray. Amen.

Majesty Above, Majesty Below

The next day, when they came down from the mountain, a large crowd met him. A man in the crowd called out, "Teacher, I beg you to look at my son, for he is my only child. A spirit seizes him and he suddenly screams; it throws him into convulsions so that he foams at the mouth. It scarcely ever leaves him and is destroying him. I begged your disciples to drive it out, but they could not."

"O unbelieving and perverse generation," Jesus replied, "how long shall I stay with you and put up with you? Bring your son here."

Even while the boy was coming, the demon threw him to the ground in a convulsion. But Jesus rebuked the evil spirit, healed the boy and gave him back to his father. And they were all amazed at the greatness of God. Luke 9:37-43

The Disciples had just witnessed Christ's inner majesty unveiled on the Mount of Transfiguration. It was the most astonishing revelation in biblical history standing beside Moses, the epitome of the Law, and Elijah, the prophets' essence. Confirm those revelations with the voice from the cloud of God's presence, and you have an experience that will light your fire.

The majestic Jesus and the three Disciples come down from the mountain to meet a crowd of people with a demonized boy at the center. Chaos reigns. Christ's majesty will now be revealed amid human misery.

As the desperate scene unfolds, a father's frantic voice cries out for his son. Seizures were destroying the boy's life. A demonic presence was killing his son, and the Disciples were helpless. Could Jesus help? Would he?

The father pleaded, "Look with mercy, Lord."

Jesus calls the boy. The devil throws the child down like a wrestler who has thrown his opponent to the mat. Christ rebukes the spirit, heals the boy, and sends him back to his father. Christ's majesty is on full display where human problems are most severe. The magnificent splendor of God the day before on the mountain is now apparent to the people below.

R. Kent Hughes says in his commentary on Luke, "Luke: That You Might Know the Truth." "We all need firsthand observations of his majesty as seen in the healing of lives–ours and others."[1] But Jesus seems frustrated by the crowd and the Disciples' inabilities to help the boy. He chastises the "unbelieving and perverse generation." Faithless people cannot deal with stubborn problems.

The boy and his father were suffering. Yet the Disciples and the people could do nothing because of their unbelief until Jesus arrived on the scene.

Jesus makes all the difference. When called upon, Christ heals the boy instantly. His majesty revealed on the mountain is now shown in the valley of despair. Verse 43 says, "They were all amazed at the greatness of God." The Greek word rendered here as "greatness" is better translated as "majesty" in the King James Version. The majesty of God is demonstrated through Jesus as he delivers people from their tragic circumstances.

Several years ago, I met a young missionary in Mexico. He was a minister who genuinely loved God. Noticing that his arms and neck were heavily tattooed, I asked about his testimony.

Growing up in California, the young man had been a gang member. Angry at the world, violence followed in his wake. Eventually, he was imprisoned and caused such problems that he was put in solitary confinement for months at a time. His only visitor was a lay minister who would stop by his cell

---

[1]   R. Kent Hughes, *Luke Volume One: That You Might Know the Truth* (Wheaton Illinois: Crossway Books, 1998), 359.

once a week. He would push a gospel tract through the small portal the staff used to deliver his food tray.

The young man did nothing but swear at the visiting minister for months. Still, the minister came week after week. Eventually, the young man looked forward to his only visitor. He started reading the tracts. One day, the prisoner asked why the lay minister kept coming. The minister told him that God loved him, and Jesus wanted to light up the young prisoner's life with his glory. With that, the young man prayed and believed in Christ as his Savior. The glory of God transformed him. I was amazed by the young missionary's testimony of God's grace found in the depths of solitary confinement. Jesus still delivers the oppressed.

Dear Lord, help my unbelief. I live in an unbelieving and perverse generation. I believe you can deliver the most difficult people and heal the impossibly sick. But I want more than that—I want to see your majesty. I ask this in Christ's name, amen.

When You Don't Know What to Do

While everyone was marveling at all that Jesus did, he said to his disciples, "Listen carefully to what I am about to tell you: The Son of Man is going to be betrayed into the hands of men." But they did not understand what this meant. It was hidden from them, so that they did not grasp it, and they were afraid to ask him about it. Luke 9: 43-45

Jesus defeated the devil, astonished the crowds, and exhilarated the disciples. Then Jesus rained on their parade. Confused, the disciples were too afraid to ask, "What's happening?"

What do you do when you don't understand what God is doing or saying?

Famed speaker and author Jack Hayford often received great compliments during his introduction before delivering his message. He responded by saying that he wished his mother were present to hear such tributes for two reasons. First, she was more deserving of any accolades, and second, she was the only one who would believe them. In the context of the people's "marveling," Christ shows us how he handled admiration–by putting it in perspective.

Jesus revealed his extraordinary nature as he healed the sick, delivered the demoniacs, raised the dead, fed the multitudes, and utterly transformed himself on the mount of Transfiguration. No wonder the crowd was amazed. Thick with enthusiasm, the air was ripe for the Messiah. But popularity is fleeting, and Jesus knew better than to trust it. He could see trouble brewing, and he warned his followers.

Betrayal is among life's most problematic experiences. The scriptures say that an honest enemy is better than a lying friend. Jesus prepared himself for the betrayal looming in Jerusalem. He seems to say, pay less attention to what people say and more attention to what they do as their actions will show you what they really think.

In Luke 9:22 Jesus explicitly warned the disciples of his inevitable suffering, death, and resurrection. He reminds them again of this reality adding the detail of his betrayal. Puzzled, the disciples don't know what to say or do.

Most people experience periods in their lives when they don't know what to do. Everything seems to go well, but this sense of foreboding disturbs their peace. Sleeplessness, lethargy, and a general lack of motivation undermines their daily activities. Welcome to the state called disappointment.

This passage shows us the worst reaction to the situation—the disciples are afraid to ask Jesus what is happening. How often in life are we afraid to ask God what to do next? Too often, confusion reigns while we wander about in the valley of fear—terrified that we will look dumb if we ask questions. Pride and fear are twin brothers that condemn us to the prison of ignorance. Luke 11:9-10 points us to answers from God:

So I say to you: Ask and it will be given to you; seek and you will find; knock and the door will be opened to you. For everyone who asks receives; he who seeks finds; and to him who knocks, the door will be opened.

Humble yourself and ask Jesus the great questions. You will find answers in the most remarkable ways. Muster the courage to seek the gifts of God that are bigger than you can imagine. Knock on God's door for the insights that will propel you down the road to new experiences and discoveries. The Lord wants us to ask for his guidance and provision.

Our body tells us to avoid suffering at all costs. Pain is no fun, and the fear of betrayal is hidden anxiety most humans harbor. Yet, Jesus seems to say, "It's coming guys. Prepare yourselves." Like the disciples, we also wonder about suffering. We sometimes question the nature of God when we see sickness, poverty, and untold pain in the world. We get serious about it when we are the ones hurting. We have a choice; we can suffer in silence, or we can ask Jesus the purpose behind the events in our lives.

What do you do when you don't know what to do? Ask. Seek. Knock. And keep on following Jesus until the answers come.

My God, I live in a bubble of ignorance— how I need your insight. I ask for wisdom to face the trials in my life. It is not my nature to ask for help, so I confess my pride today, humble myself, and come to you. Please help me, Lord, to understand what happened to you and what is happening to me. In the name of Jesus, I pray. Amen.

The Greatest

An argument started among the disciples as to which of them would be the greatest. Jesus, knowing their thoughts, took a little child and had him stand beside him. Then he said to them, "Whoever welcomes this little child in my name welcomes me; and whoever welcomes me welcomes the one who sent me. For he who is least among you all — he is the greatest."

"Master," said John, "we saw a man driving out demons in your name and we tried to stop him, because he is not one of us."

"Do not stop him," Jesus said, "for whoever is not against you is for you." Luke 9:46-50

Since my dad left when I was five years old, I have been on this unconscious quest to succeed and recover what was lost. Generally, we want to feel loved, respected, and admired. Ambitions drive us to heart attacks. Intellectual and scientific pursuits push us past reasonable boundaries. Entertainment and sports dominate our attention as they give us the feeling of achievement, even if it is through someone else. Most people want to feel they are great.

Picture the scene here as the Disciples argue over who is the greatest while Jesus plays with a child. He is seemingly oblivious to the Disciple's debate. Christ's followers contend about who is the greatest among them. The discussion was more severe than they let on. Each of them longed to be top dog.

Jesus interrupts the Disciples with his teaching in the moment. Holding the child close, the Lord attempts to refocus their vision. He seems to say, "Love matters, status stinks. Joy rules. Rivalry rots the bones. Ladder climbing wears you out, while play renews your strength. Look at the child, brothers."

By most earthly standards, a child is unimportant—no money, possessions, property, or fame. They are virtually powerless. Yet Christ exemplifies the child as the greatest among them.

Why?

In their simplicity they welcome Jesus, "he said to them, 'Whoever welcomes this little child in my name welcomes me,'" (verse 48). Children play with almost anybody—even the bearded Savior who speaks in mysteries. If we simply took the time to welcome Jesus and spent time with him, we would be better people.

Jesus nailed the vanity of the Disciples, so how do they react?

Like us, they use their faithful old friend–deflection. They pivot to another topic and whine, "Well, Jesus, that guy over there is casting out demons, and he isn't even with us." It was their way of saying they were at least better than those people.

What's wrong with the Disciples craving to be the greatest? In their desire for recognition as Christ's real followers, they were oblivious to the human needs around them. Somehow, they were not aware of the child that Jesus found. They also missed the plight of the demon-possessed person that other people delivered in verse 49. Fortunately, someone ministered to the man, even though he "is not one of us." In their quest to feel superior, they lost sight of the plight of people.

Are we like the disciples in the depth of our souls?

Do we long for status to make us feel significant?

Do we believe we are Christ's exclusive followers because that makes us feel better than others?

Down deep, the notion we are insignificant haunts us. In our own eyes, we fear our lives are meaningless.

Thomas Aquinas wrote, "Fear is such a powerful emotion for humans, that when we allow it to take us over, it drives compassion right out of our hearts." Fear and pride tear at the fabric of Christianity just as they consumed the disciples. Competing theologies birth division. Ministries striving to be the biggest and the best are born of the desire to be the greatest. Denominations warring to protect their turf are the scourge of modern Christianity.

Standing not far away, Jesus holds the child. Imagine Jesus looking at his disciples and shaking his head. "Look at this child," he seems to say to us. Neither striving nor jockeying for position. The little child stands innocent, vulnerable, and open–the ideal follower.

My youngest daughter is a bartender at a high-end restaurant in the Boston area. She works with many people with alternative lifestyles. Gays, lesbians, transgender people, and non-gender folks each carry baggage from their life stories. She recently said that she would never identify herself to them as a born-again, evangelical Christian because those terms would evoke images of judgmental or political associations.

"How do you identify yourself with them?" I asked her.

"I tell them I'm with Jesus," She said.

That simple phrase releases the power to spread the grace Christ came to give away. No condemnation, no indoctrination, no competition, and no finger-wagging, just Jesus.

John 1:12-13 adds, "Yet to all who received him (Jesus), to those who believed in his name, he gave the right to become children of God." In the end, it is those who become like children that are the greatest of all.

Father God, I believe I am your child. Please help me act like one. I want to shed my ambition and cease striving. I am so tired of trying to win the approval of people. I open myself to you so we can enjoy one another. Forgive me for trying to exalt myself before others. In Jesus' name, I pray. Amen.

The Road Through Hostility

As the time approached for him to be taken up to heaven, Jesus resolutely set out for Jerusalem. And he sent messengers on ahead, who went into a Samaritan village to get things ready for him; but the people there did not welcome him, because he was heading for Jerusalem. When the disciples James and John saw this, they asked, "Lord, do you want us to call fire down from heaven to destroy them?" But Jesus turned and rebuked them, and they went to another village. Luke 9:51-56

Heroes face their problems truthfully, even at the risk of personal loss. At the peak of His popularity,

Christ turns His face "resolutely" toward Jerusalem's hostile environment. While we work at avoiding adversity, Jesus marches straight toward it. His Disciples' responses along the way foreshadow the opposition Christ faced head-on.

In the previous passage, Jesus corrected his disciples when they concerned themselves with who would be the greatest among them. They also missed the point when they saw others ministering to a demon-oppressed person. Now, the disciples strike out again in Luke 9:51-56. We learn a great deal through the disciple's failures, and this one is relevant.

Christ turns toward hostile Jerusalem, and their route takes them through despised Samaria. The Jews shunned the Samaritans because historically, they intermarried with pagan nations. The most conservative in the Jewish culture believed that] perverted the Jewish religious beliefs. The road to Jerusalem ran through Samaria, so the Disciples sought accommodations there. Denied by the Samaritans, Christ's disciples wanted to call down hellfire to destroy those disagreeable half-breed Samaritans.

Really?

Jesus must have shaken his head as he rebuked the Disciples for their vengeful and discriminatory attitudes. Jesus was on the road destined for a cruel cross to purchase our salvation, and his Disciples wanted to burn those who inconvenienced them with eternal fire. The Lord rebuked them yet again.

Christ wants to lead us to emotional adulthood, and this journey will take us through adversity and hostility. I am ashamed when I remember how many times I have reacted angrily to disagreeable people. If we abandon striving and competition to return to the simplicity of childlike innocence, we will have peaceful relationships. Understanding that those who are different are not the enemy could introduce us to new friends if we accept them. Albert Schweitzer said, "Constant kindness can accomplish much. As the sun makes ice melt, kindness causes misunderstanding, mistrust, and hostility to evaporate." Christ's mission would lead Him through hostility to become the greatest peacemaker in the history of the world.

Rudyard Kipling immortalized the spirit of Christ's character in his poem "If." It states

If you can keep your head when all around you are losing theirs and blaming it on you; if you can trust yourself when all men doubt you but make allowance for their doubting too; if you can wait and not be tired by waiting, or being lied about, don't deal in lies, or being hated don't give way to hating...Yours is the Earth and everything that's in it...

It is not those who call down judgment on others, but it's the peacemakers who change the world.

The Disciples viewed the Samaritans as people who corrupted their Jewish doctrines and traditions, despising them for it. Fighting among Christians does the same thing. Catholics, Protestants, and Orthodox all warred for centuries in Europe. Doctrinal and denominational quarreling plague American Christianity to this day. Each contends to be right.

"Shall we call down fire from heaven?" we seem to say with the same spirit as the disciples. God help us.

As I neared the end of writing my first book, "Every Day Jesus," I made an astonishing discovery—there are no theological or denominational controversies in the Gospel of Luke. The only hostility that Jesus faces is from religious people bound by their theological systems.

The Pharisees, Christ's primary adversaries, were like modern-day evangelicals and Pentecostals. The Pharisees believed in the literal Word of God and sought to live in obedience to the Law of Moses. They were so zealous they created a system of rules to protect people from coming close to disobeying the Laws of the Torah. But their practices had become more important than God's Word.

The Sadducees, Christ's other adversaries, liberally intellectualized the Torah so they could justify their positions of wealth and power. They arrayed themselves against Jesus because they felt he threatened the status quo.

The disciples offered to call down fire from heaven to judge the Samaritans and thus showed the same judgmental spirit as the Pharisees and the Sadducees. Christ rejects their offer because he did not come into the world to condemn us.

Jesus did not become human to judge our lifestyles or our theological systems. He came to show us the way back to God. He didn't use religious tests, denominational standards, or theological methods to do it. Jesus travels the road through hostility to demonstrate the ways of the Lord are neither vengeful nor judgmental. They focus solely on God.

> *Lord God, thank you for Jesus. Deliver me from the plagues of religion and judgementalism. Fill me with your grace, peace, and forgiveness that I might show who you are to the world. I pray this in the name of Jesus. Amen.*

How to Stop Procrastinating

As they were walking along the road, a man said to him, "I will follow you wherever you go."

Jesus replied, "Foxes have holes and birds of the air have nests, but the Son of Man has no place to lay his head."

He said to another man, "Follow me."

But the man replied, "Lord, first let me go and bury my father."

Jesus said to him, "Let the dead bury their own dead, but you go and proclaim the kingdom of God."

Still another said, "I will follow you, Lord; but first let me go back and say good-by to my family."

Jesus replied, "No one who puts his hand to the plow and looks back is fit for service in the kingdom of God." Luke 9:57-62

Too many excuses delay our growth.

Three people in this story have three different excuses before entering Christ's service. The first was discouraged that there was no plan for his physical comfort, no Marriott Hotels on Jesus' path to Jerusalem. The second wanted first to take care of his family, then follow Christ. The third was a relational fellow who wanted to "say goodbye" to his family.

All the explanations were reasonable, yet Christ was on a life and death mission that would change the course of eternity. Jesus saw the big picture. He knew what had to get done that day. Will we follow Jesus even when we don't understand what he is doing? Or will we do as the Lord asks even when it inconveniences us in some way?

Many Christians are discouraged by their lack of obedience. We know what we should be doing, but the business of life pressures us. We go to bed exhausted at night realizing we didn't do the most important things. Christ gives us the impulse to do something good, but on the way, we get distracted. Procrastination robs us of God's best when we miss his timing.

Recently, I've discovered a simple rule that helps crush the power of delay. I call it the "two-minute rule." The goal is to make it easier to get started on the things we should be doing. The rule is, "start now, do it for at least two minutes, and implement that discipline in your life daily."

Most of the tasks that we procrastinate doing aren't difficult to do. We have the talent and skills to accomplish them. We just avoid starting them.

There are two parts to the idea, "Part One says if it takes less than two minutes, then do it now." This imperative originally comes from David Allen's bestselling book, "Getting Things Done." Apply this principle to your spiritual life. Imagine waking up in the morning and praying for two minutes. You will sense the presence of the Lord, and that changes everything.

Part Two of the Two-Minute Rule is, "When you start a new habit, it should take less than two minutes to do." Can your goals be accomplished in less than two minutes? No, but most plans can be started in two minutes.

Take the first step. It might sound like this strategy is too basic for your grand life plans. Still, I submit that it works for any goal because of one simple reason—in the words of internet blogger James Clears, "the physics of real life."

Sir Isaac Newton taught us a long time ago, objects at rest tend to stay at rest, and objects in motion tend to stay in motion. This principle is as true for humans as it is for falling apples. The Two–Minute Rule works for both big and small goals because of the inertia of life. Once you start doing something, it's easier to continue doing it. The focus is on taking action and letting things flow from there.

I believe the Lord is calling people us to work in His kingdom. It might be to stop and pray for two minutes. Or say a kind word to a neighbor. He may be calling us to follow Him in a particular ministry or to solve world hunger. I know that nothing will happen until we take a step of faith. God created the "inertia of life" in nature, and it will work for us if we just get underway.

Do you want to be a praying Christian? You can. Try two minutes now. Do you desire to read through the complete Bible? You can try two minutes of reading right now and plan to do that each day. Don't beat yourself up if you miss a day. Carry on the following day.

I can't guarantee "The Two Minute Rule" will work for you. But I promise that it will not work if you never try. What's something positive you can do that will take you less than two minutes? Do it right now. Put your hand to the plow. Begin to live the Christian life you always wanted.

Lord Jesus, too often I act like the three people in this passage. I have too many reasons why I can't do what you are urging me to do. Forgive me, Lord. Help me stay on your tasks. You said that your yoke is easy, and your burden is light. Yet why do I fear it so? I ask for the courage to take on your yoke of discipline and work it. I ask for a plan to follow you every day. Help me to start now for at least two minutes. I pray these things in your name. Amen.

Extraordinary Jesus, Extraordinary Followers

As they were walking along the road, a man said to him, "I will follow you wherever you go."

Jesus replied, "No one who puts his hand to the plow and looks back is fit for service in the kingdom of God." Luke 9:62

Jesus walked the earth as a normal person—an ordinary man—with human feelings and needs. Yet, He was also exceptional. He had that extra something that empowered him to attain something beyond the ordinary. Jesus was, is, and always will be extraordinary.

Turn your gaze toward heaven and open your arms wide to receive an extraordinary Savior. Take a deep breath of the Spirit of Jesus. Suck in the rare air of the Kingdom of God. Your life will slowly transform into extraordinary.

We have walked with Christ down the dusty roads of Northern Israel. Remember all that you have seen—ten miracles in the last forty days. Jesus is like the second coming of Moses, yet so much more. Compare the wonders of Moses with those of the Lord in Luke 8-9:

- Christ crossed the Galilee and spoke, "peace to the storm." Moses called down storms of hail and lightning on Egypt.
- Jesus delivered a man possessed by a multitude of demons named "Legion." Moses confronted an empire obsessed with a pantheon of gods.
- Christ sends the freedman back to his hometown to witness to the grace of God while Moses led the Children of Israel out of Egypt to discover the Promised Land.
- Jesus healed the woman with the issue of blood, but Moses turned the Nile river into blood.
- Jesus raised Jairus's daughter from the dead while Moses pronounced the judgment of death upon Egypt's firstborn.

- Christ commissioned his seventy disciples to heal the sick, and Moses appointed seventy elders of Israel.
- Jesus ministered to all who were afflicted. To heal the diseased, Moses lifted the pole with the serpent, and they recovered.
- Christ fed the multitudes with 12 baskets leftover, and Moses fed the people manna from heaven, but no extra pieces.
- Christ transfigured on the holy mountain, and Moses glowed with the glory of God after the presence of God passed by.
- Jesus healed the deaf and mute boy while Moses leads a people who do not want to hear God's voice.

The Disciples experienced so much as they followed Christ throughout Galilee. Then, Jesus changed direction, pivoting toward Jerusalem and certain doom. Who will follow him now?

The Disciples were at the tipping point, the crucial crossroad where a wrong turn would cast them headlong into the deep, dark hole of forgettable history. Or they could choose to risk their lives pursuing the will of God. No middle ground.

The Scriptures above outline the challenge. Believers must follow Jesus wherever he leads, challenged to move forward without regrets. In Luke 9:62, using The Passion Translation (TPT), Jesus says, "Why do you keep looking backward to your past and have second thoughts about following me? When you turn back you are useless to God's kingdom realm." Living with regret is like driving with your eyes continually looking in the rearview mirror—crashing is inevitable.

As we conclude these forty days following Christ through the Gospel of Luke, we plunge forward in the way of the Master. We can walk in his steps in our time.

Will we choose to follow him even when it costs us or inconveniences us?

Even when our livelihoods are in danger?

Even when it forces us to prioritize the Kingdom of God, above all else?

After graduating from Life Pacific College in 1979, I set out from Los Angeles toward my first ministry assignment in Bradford, Pennsylvania, deep in the Allegheny Mountains. My wife, newborn baby girl, and I drove our Chevy pulling a small U-Haul trailer with all our earthly possessions. Traveling east from L.A. on Interstate 10, we hit the Arizona state line. It suddenly felt like someone lifted a heavy backpack off my shoulders.

I realized I no longer carried the weight of responsibility for our lives. We were following God and trusting that he would take care of us. While I have seen many heartbreaking challenges, following Jesus has been a fantastic ride.

I agree with King David, who said in Psalm 37:25, "I was young and now I am old, yet I have never seen the righteous forsaken or their children begging bread." Following Jesus has been the most extraordinary adventure.

The Lord confronts us to leave everything, then provides an amazing abundance. He commands his followers to abandon the world and then gives us more than we could have imagined. Christ tells us not to look back and imparts to us a vision of the future. Jesus is that extraordinary. Will you be an extraordinary follower?

Lord God, thank you for the exciting journey you have called me to walk. I pray for the courage to follow you even when the way is hard. I choose to pursue you wholeheartedly with no looking back, no regrets. Jesus, you are indeed the way, the truth, and the life. You are my life. May your kingdom come, your will be done on earth as it is in heaven. Amen.

A Word to Church Leaders

Pastors, this devotional speaks to the guys and gals you lead who want to know Jesus. Most of them care little about the nuances of faith over which we who trained in Bible college or seminary tend to obsess.

Use this simple work to teach those faith-filled people to employ the ways of Christ as a pattern for discipleship. By recommending this book to your people you will help them establish a life-long practice of reading the Bible and praying daily.

Having pastored for more than thirty-eight years, I have often observed ministers and denominations using starchy prescriptions for new believers. The standard line goes:

- *read the Bible*
- *pray*
- *go to church*
- *tithe*
- *be faithful members*
- *serve tirelessly*
- *give to missions.*

While those are good convictions, are we inventing a new Christian code? Have we created a reward system for knowing Jesus? Are we putting yokes of structure and institutionalism on people that make them grow weary?

These activities inhibit Christian growth when they become systematized rather than being relationship-based. When people feel they must measure up to certain standards for acceptance they lose sight of the unconditional acceptance they are given through Jesus.

I believe our mandate is more significant. The supreme commands Christ gave us are to love God and love one another. Our lives and faith must flow from these instructions. Our church communities will pulsate with life when these are the priorities.

Many people of faith are tired of *Churchianity* but crave a real relationship with Jesus. This devotional speaks to that hunger.

Pastor, imagine the believers in your fellowship reading and praying their way through the life of Jesus. People become like the object of their attention. By centering their lives on Christ daily, they become like him. The results are strong, stable, balanced, fire-breathing believers in Christ.

I came to faith in Christ during the height of the *Jesus Movement* in 1970 at Angelus Temple, the International Church of the Foursquare Gospel headquarters. That church exposed me to many great leaders such as Jack Hayford, Paul (David) Yonggi Cho, David du Plessis, Chuck Smith, Josh McDowell, and Bill Bright. These mentors invested more spiritual dynamic in my life than I can ever repay. They showed me the depths of God's Word, the power of his Spirit, and the breadth of his great love for the world.

I am an evangelical who graduated *Magna Cum Laude* from Gordon-Conwell Theological Seminary in South Hamilton, Massachusetts with a Master of Arts degree. I'm honored that the Rev. Billy Graham signed my diploma. I treasure my training as it gave me the tools I needed to study the scriptures in depth. Nonetheless, I once heard theologian and philosopher Francis Schaeffer say that a real intellectual can put truth in terms an ordinary person can understand. That is my goal, and I pray is yours as well.

This book is not merely an inspirational devotional like *Our Daily Bread* or *Jesus Calling*. Devotionals like that are helpful but very brief as they provide 200-300 words per day and require only a few moments of the reader's time. Extraordinary

Jesus includes 800-1,000 words per day and challenges the reader to read the scripture in context and pray specifically applying the truths found there.

I hope to bring depth and focus on Christ's life directly from Luke's Gospel in sequential order. Gordon Fee's *How to Read the Bible for All Its Worth* guided my efforts as it shows the importance of interpreting the scriptures in context. I pray this devotional interprets Bible truths in their original context and then applies them to modern life.

Extraordinary Jesus, and my previous book *Every Day Jesus,* are designed to walk believers event by event, paragraph by paragraph, through Christ's life. I pray that sound exegesis undergirds each chapter. May the power of Christ's Spirit release spiritual energy to help the reader grow in their faith!

Extraordinary Jesus is the second of a series of devotionals, gently leading believers through the life of Christ in the Gospel of Luke. More than anything, I pray that the people who read *Extraordinary Jesus* become like Jesus. I pray that this Jesus journey assists church leaders in the great challenge of teaching people to love like Christ, to walk with him, and to be Jesus to the world.

Bibliography

Aland, Kurt, ed. 1985. *Synopsis of the Four Gospels.* New York: United Bible Societies.

Amoral, Joe. 2011. *Understanding Jesus, Cultural Insights into the Words and Deeds of Christ.* New York, NY: Faith Words.

Anderson, Leith. 2005 *Jesus, An Intimate Portrait of the Man, His Land, and His People.* Minneapolis, MN: Bethany House.

Barclay, William. 1956. *The Gospel of Luke, The Daily Study Bible Series.* Philadelphia, PA: The Westminster Press.

Buckingham, Jamie. 1991. *Parables, Poking Holes in Religious Balloons.* Lake Mary, FL: Creation House.

Childers, Charles L., 1971. *The Gospel According to St. Luke, Beacon Bible Commentary.* Kansas City, Missouri: Beacon Hill Press.

Courson, Jon. 2003. *Application Commentary.* Nashville, TN: Thomas Nelson.

Edersheim, Alfred. 1905. *The Life and Times of Jesus the Messiah.* New York, NY: Longman's, Green, and Co.

Erdman, Charles R., 1975. *The Gospel of Luke.* Philadelphia, PA: The Westminster Press.

France, R.T., 2013. *Luke, Teach the Text Series.* Grand Rapids, MI: Baker Books.

Geldenhuys, Norval. 1983. *The Gospel of Luke, The New International Commentary on the New Testament.* Grand Rapids, MI: Wm. B. Eerdmans Publishing Company.

The Holy Bible: New International Version. 1984. Colorado Springs, Co: International Bible Society.

Hughes, R. Kent. 1998. *Luke, Volume 1, That You May Know the Truth*. Wheaton, IL: Crossway Books.

Jenkins, Jerry B., Lahaye, Tim. 2009. *Luke's Story, by Faith Alone*. New York, NY: Putnam Praise, G.P. Punam's Sons.

Johnson, Luke Timothy. 2011. *Prophetic Jesus, Prophetic Church*. Grand Rapids, MI: William B. Eerdmans Publishing Company.

LaSor, William Sanford. 1961. *Great Personalities of the New Testament, Their Lives and Times*. Westwood, NJ: Fleming H. Revell Company.

Lucado, Max. 2002. *Just Like Jesus, a Thirty Day Walk With the Savior*. Nashville, TN: Thomas Nelson.

Moore, Beth. 2007. *Jesus, 90 Days With the One and Only*. Nashville, TN: B&H Publishing Group.

Morgan, G. Campbell. 1943. The Parables and Metaphors of Our Lord. Old Tappan, NJ: Fleming H. Revell Company.

Morris, Leon. 1974. *Luke, Tyndale New Testament Commentaries*. Grand Rapids, MI: William B. Eerdman's Publishing.

Muggeridge, Malcolm. 1975. *Jesus, The Man Who Lives*. New York, NY: Harper & Row Publishers.

Nouwen, Henri. 2001. *Jesus, A Gospel*. Maryknoll, NY: Orbis Books.

Ogilvie, Lloyd John. 1979. *Autobiography of God, God Revealed in the Parables of Jesus.* Ventura, CA: Regal Books.

Peterson, Eugene H., 1993. *The Message.* Colorado Springs, CO: Navpress.

Renner, Rick. 2003. *Sparkling Gems from the Greek.* Tulsa, OK: Harrison House Publishing.

Stronstad, Roger. 2012. *The Charismatic Theology of St. Luke.* Grand Rapids, MI: Baker Academic.

Trench, R.C. 1977. *Notes on the Parables of Our Lord.* Grand Rapids, MI: Baker Book House.

Wangerin, Walter Jr., 2005. *Jesus, A Novel.* Grand Rapids, MI: Zondervan.

Wieland, Albert Cassel. 1947. A New Harmony of the Gospels. Grand Rapids, Michigan: Wm. B. Eerdmans Publishing Co.

Zodhiates, Spiro. 1990. *The Hebrew-Greek Key Study Bible.* Chattanooga, TN: AMG Publishers.

ABOUT THE AUTHOR

 Dave Holland lives to help people become more like Jesus. His life mission is to *love God and love people*. He pastored churches for over 38 years and learned that the church and Jesus are not the same. He has been serving God for 50 years and found that Jesus is the only true foundation for life.

Pastor Dave planted a thriving church in Brockton, Massachusetts. Starting with just sixteen people, the church grew, and from that church, he launched seven other congregations in New England. He also led a church in Uxbridge, Massachusetts, as well as pastoring in Nebraska and Colorado.

After graduating from Life Pacific College in 1979, the International Church of the Foursquare Gospel ordained him in 1981. While pastoring in New England, he earned his Master of Arts Degree from Gordon-Conwell Theological Seminary, where he graduated Magnum Cum Laude in 1997. He says of his seminary experience, "God spoke to me the first day I attended classes that 'education tends to pride, study hard but don't let it go to your head.'"

Extraordinary Jesus

He also graduated with a Master of Arts degree in English from Grand Canyon University in 2019.

Dave studied the Gospel of Luke for over ten years while writing the first book in the *Daily Jesus* Series. *Christmas Jesus* is the first installment, followed by *Every Day Jesus,* covering the first four chapters of Luke. This book speaks from Luke chapters 5-9. With the Lord's help Dave plans to publish *Prodigal Jesus*, covering Luke chapters 10-15, in 2021.

Thanks for joining us on this journey to know Jesus every day.

You can learn more about Dave on his website, DaveHolland.org or email him at davidvholland54@gmail.com if you have questions.

Made in the USA
Columbia, SC
02 March 2023